Mindfulness:

A Better Me; A Better You; A Better World

Mindfulness:
A Better Me; A Better You; A Better World

Annabel Beerel, PhD
and Tom Raffio, FLMI

To Betsy,

Wishing you a mindful life!

Annabel

Dedications

To my Father, a remarkable man and a very special Dad.

– Annabel

Thank you to my mother, my sisters, my children: Jenna, Matt, Brian, Gabbie, Annika, Margaret, and Sophie, and most especially to my lovely wife, Ellen, for her unconditional love and continuous support of my mindfulness journey. Thank you for being you.

– Tom

Annabel and Tom also wish to thank the team at Northeast Delta Dental who have so enthusiastically and consistently engaged in Mindful and Meditation practices and have so generously shared their experiences.

Contents

Chapter 3
The Benefits of Mindfulness

Chapter 4
The Mind and The Brain

Chapter 5
Meditation: The Foundation of Mindfulness

Chapter 6
Mindful Leadership

Chapter 7
Mindfulness—A Change Initiative

Chapter 8
Managing Organizations and Mindful Virtues

Chapter 9
Putting Mindfulness To Work — Part 1:
Communication Strategies

Chapter 10
Putting Mindfulness To Work—Part 2:
Performance Strategies

Foreword

This is a very special and important book. It is a book everyone should read. It has been carefully crafted to explain in clear and simple language what mindfulness is and its huge importance to the quality of our lives, especially during these challenging times.

This is also a highly practical book. It is filled with stories and examples from around the world and from within one of New Hampshire's consistently Best Companies to Work for—Northeast Delta Dental—which also has been selected as one of the 25 best companies to work for in America.

I am not surprised that Tom Raffio, president and CEO of Northeast Delta Dental is the co-author of this exciting new book. As long as I have known Tom he has always been ahead of his time. He enjoys embracing new ideas and is practical and down to earth. I am delighted that Tom has collaborated with a distinguished colleague Annabel Beerel, PhD to write a book on mindfulness. He is a mindful leader. He listens, chooses his words carefully and thoughtfully and is a great leader in many ways. His visionary foresight for companies that he is involved with, along with his ability to pay attention to the details, has earned him many significant recognitions and awards. He always leaves an organization better than he found it.

Tom is a graduate of Harvard University and has an MBA from Babson College. He is a Fellow of the Life Management Institute. He is a member of the Leadership New Hampshire Class of 1997. Tom has been in the insurance industry all of his working life and has been involved in the Delta Dental organization for over thirty years. Over the past twenty plus years he has been guiding and growing

Northeast Delta Dental to new heights of success. He firmly believes that in order to be successful, you need first to be a good corporate citizen and be involved in Municipal and State matters in your service area. He has been an active member of numerous boards and has held numerous leadership positions on those boards. He is perhaps best known for chairing the New Hampshire State Board of Education for ten years. His belief that knowledge is the key to success and helps foster stronger leaders has proliferated through all grades. He continues to mentor individuals and organizations to ensure that our State remains strong going forward.

His amazing work within his company and in his community has earned him many well deserved honors and distinctions. These include Business Leader of the Year by the Association of New Hampshire Chambers of Commerce Executives and Business New Hampshire Magazine in 2004, Business Leader of the Decade in 2010, Leadership in the Arts by the New Hampshire Business Committee for the Arts 2005. The National Alliance on Mental Illness presented him with the Samuel Adams Community Leadership Award in 2007. Pastoral Counseling Services of Manchester honored him with the Good Samaritan Award in 2008. The Greater Concord Chamber of Commerce selected Tom at its Citizen of the Year and then Governor John Lynch proclaimed November 16, 2009, as Tom Raffio Day in New Hampshire.

Tom practices what he preaches and is a determined advocate for health and fitness for citizens of all ages. Delta Dental sponsors many road races and general wellness programs throughout northern New England. He is an exercise fanatic and races in over one hundred annual events. He has been known to run up mountains, including Mt. Washington. His wife, Ellen, shares his passion and runs with him in these races.

In 2013, Tom co-authored *There are No Do-Overs: The Big Red Factors for Sustaining a Business Long Term* with NBA Hall of Famer, Dave Cowens and former Northeast Delta Dental colleague, Barbara McLaughlin.

Tom's co-author, Annabel Beerel, PhD, has an outstanding record of achievement in her own right. Besides her intriguing multi-faceted international background, Annabel has worked with top organizations in the U.S. and abroad. She is well known in New Hampshire and Massachusetts for her New England Women's Leadership Institute and her interests in empowering women. She is an effective change agent and has worked with many organizations around mergers and acquisitions. More recently her focus has been on introducing the concept of mindfulness. She is an accomplished speaker on varied topics and a prolific writer. Tom and Annabel are indeed a formidable team.

I highly recommend that you read this powerful and timely book.

- Dr. Sylvio L. Dupuis

It Is All In The Mind

A PASSION FOR THE MIND

As a young girl, I had a special relationship with my father. He loved to teach me things. One of my father's favorite phrases was "It is all in the mind!" My father was a philosopher in his own way. Even though he was a highly pragmatic man, he grounded his life in certain foundational philosophies that formed a coherent system that shaped his view of the world.

My father believed adamantly that the way we look at things—our attitude, our disposition, our willingness to be open to new possibilities—was one of the greatest gifts to humanity, and that it was up to each one of us to maximize this gift. Of course, as his daughter, I was subjected to these lessons frequently.

The only way to live life to the fullest, my father believed, was to have the right disposition. If disappointing events or unpleasant situations occurred, I was encouraged to consciously and actively use my mind to decide how I was going to view these events, and how I was going to respond to them. Whenever I would complain or bemoan something, he would frequently say: "Annabel, it is all in the mind." If I was upset, disappointed or afraid, he would give me a serious yet loving look, and say: "Annabel, it is how you look at it. Change your mind!"

Whenever I came home from school feeling disappointed or dejected, my father would counsel me to take heart. He would begin as always with, "It is not so bad. Try to look at it a little differently.

If you change your mind you will see that it will pass and tomorrow will be another day." I thank him for these insights daily.

I can also never be grateful enough for the passion for learning that my father instilled in me. He taught me to fly a small plane, how to play chess, how to read music, the beauty of horses, and a passion for tennis. As I write these lines, I can see him sitting in front of me, puffing his pipe, scratching his balding head, and stroking my arm gently; something he loved to do.

LEARNING HOW WE THINK

My life's journey has taken many twists and turns. I have lived and worked in several continents and many countries. The one thing that keeps both pulling me forward and pushing me from behind is the idea that it is all in the mind. Everything we do and experience is a function of the quality of our minds.

After training as a chartered accountant in South Africa and working for several large conglomerates that dominated the South African industrial scene, in the early 1980s I left for London, England. There I completed my MBA specializing in finance and strategic planning. At the time, I had a strange notion that I wanted to be a corporate financier and investment banker. I tried it and found it was not a good fit for my temperament or my soul.

A Thinking Opportunity

Through a remarkable set of circumstances, I grabbed an opportunity to learn how to develop Artificial Intelligence (AI) systems. Now therein lies a story (and three books). I was charged by my company with developing a PC-based expert system that simulated the expertise of a corporate lending expert. At that time, I was doing a great deal of advising to small and growing businesses on how to construct their business plans and how to finance their growth. I knew all about leverage and loans and, thanks to a wide range of incredible experiences as an accountant, a lot about businesses.

The challenge for me was that I had to design the system, act as the main expert, and write the computer code. And I did it! My father would have been proud.

The most relevant part of this story to our discussions is that in designing AI or expert systems, one is replicating the thinking process of an expert or experts. This means one must have some knowledge of how we think and process our thoughts, and then how different actions follow as a result.

You can imagine how much I had to learn. I was not a cognitive psychologist or a neuroscientist. I was an MBA, good at math, who had some facility with computers. So began my detailed study of the mind, consciousness, thinking, judgment, decision-making and problem-solving strategies. It was an immersion to the extreme—and how exhilarating!

My computer prototype was a huge success. It actually worked! Even more impressive, it could outperform many people carrying out the corporate lending function. By outperform, I mean its assessment of the risk of a loan was more accurate and thorough than that carried out by many of the supposed banking experts. This did not exactly make me popular with some folks.

You can imagine that I learned many huge lessons along the way. These lessons include:
- Few people, even so-called experts, think about how they think
- Many people are unaware of the heuristic strategies (rules of thumb) they use to justify decisions
- Rules of thumb become ingrained and are rarely challenged, even if they are outdated or inappropriate for a specific decision
- People are usually not good at explaining why they selected a certain course of action. They justify their rationale after the event
- Value judgments play a huge role in decision-making. Most people are not aware or conscious of how significant this is

- By and large we all struggle with uncertainty and tend to default to fear, risk aversion, and defensive options
- Many people hailed as experts are not creative. They have simply mastered decision-making in a limited domain. Relying on them for new developments leads to disappointment
- Few people are aware, present, and conscious of their thinking, feelings, and intuition in the present moment. They think and act mechanically

Watch Out!

The experience I have just described totally changed my life. I became very interested in my own consciousness and my own thinking. Talk about a wake-up call that continues daily.

While my computer system was a technical success, it was not welcomed by many managers. The fear of being replaced by a machine — this was in the 1990s — provided enormous barriers of resistance. The more progressive organizations realized the opportunities, and so my AI company was born.

One exciting finding for me was that, once people had an opportunity to "play" with the system, and to query its expertise, they became more interested and less afraid. Here was an opportunity for them to see a decision-path towards a choice and to compare it with their own. Now they were hooked. Did they think like this? What could they learn? How might they hone their thinking capabilities? Maybe they could become better decision-makers if they became more mindful of their moment-to-moment, day-by-day thoughts and behavior.

As we know, more and more of these systems are going to pervade our lives. While a machine — no matter how clever — will never replace the magnificence of the human mind, it can replace our mechanical habitual behaviors. We had better watch out!

A Beautiful Mind

Over the years I have consulted with many, many organizations in a variety of domains. My interest is in leadership and change, ethics, group dynamics, and of course mindfulness. In all these areas of engagement, I am intrigued by how people apply their minds (or don't), how they understand reality, wherein lies their impetus to do things, the role of the will, the source of courage and determination, and the moment of choice.

I have studied comparative religions, comparative ethics, the mystical traditions, consciousness, spiritual psychology, and mindfulness and meditation. They all have a great deal to say about the mind, awareness, and how we construe reality.

I bring this collage of experiences to our discussions in this book. I hope that in my sharing, they provide helpful insights, and that if nothing else, they ignite a passion in you to learn about the mystery and magnificence of your own mind. It is beautiful.

OUR PARTNERSHIP

I met Tom Raffio, President & CEO of Northeast Delta Dental (Delta Dental), ten years ago. At the time, I held an Ethics Chair at a New Hampshire university and had an opportunity to carry out ethics training with his employees. From the beginning, working with Delta Dental was a pleasure. The people were engaged and smart, the culture was open and collegial, and the leadership and management were excellent.

I have been fortunate to be engaged by Delta Dental frequently over the years. Tom invariably comes to say hello during a class or seminar, and personally supports all training and development. Over the years, I have marveled at the depth and range of education and training Delta Dental provides its employees.

When it came to my deciding whom to partner with in writing this book, Tom was the immediate choice. He is one of the most open and forward-thinking people I know. There was no hesitation. I was already working with him by bringing mindfulness into the Delta Dental culture. So, here we are, sharing our experiences, and lessons learned, with you.

TOM'S PERSPECTIVE

No business can succeed if its employees are not happy and engaged because unhappy employees create unhappy customers. So one of my goals since becoming President and CEO of Northeast Delta Dental (Delta Dental) in 1995 has been to focus on the well-being of our employees. Our leadership team has worked to guide, support and engage our team members, and our efforts have paid off. Not only do we have extraordinarily loyal and productive employees, we have been voted *One of the Ten Best Companies to Work for in New Hampshire* many times and have been in the Hall of Fame twice as a result.

The things we at Delta Dental have worked on have evolved over time. In the early days, we focused on adding traditional benefits like insurance. Then we worked on skills training and career advancement. Then it was work/life balance and flex time. Today? It is stress management and how to handle the multiple demands on our time. Fortunately, there is a solution: mindfulness, which teaches us to relax, focus on one thing at a time, be in the moment, really listen, and respond mindfully.

We need to help our employees be less stressed while being more productive. In conversations with the other Best Companies leaders at various business and social events, we remark on the growing stress of trying to do too many things without doing one thing in a first class manner. For instance, we may actually delude ourselves into thinking we are accomplishing a lot by answering 100 emails a day, when over 90 may add no value to the customer. We confuse quantity of work with quality of work. If top tier companies such as Delta Dental are suffering this blight, what about start-ups or struggling companies?

The culprit behind our stress may be multitasking brought on by poor use of technology. As we have all made greater and greater use of technology, which we believe will make us more efficient, we find ourselves multitasking as never before. We answer emails while talking on the phone. We text while in meetings. We can't even walk without our mobile devices. A year or so ago, I started to observe the frenetic pace craziness in my business and personal life—employee colleagues multitasking, family members texting while at the dinner table, Board members emailing while in the middle of a Board meeting, and people in general bragging about their ability to multitask. I started to notice poor grammar or poorly written emails from my normally stellar employee colleagues when they tried to compose emails while talking to a customer on the phone. In my own life, I actually noticed a ringing in my ears when I was multitasking.

One day I drove the 15 minutes home from work while participating in a (hands free) teleconference with my Board. I arrived home and the teleconference ended, but I couldn't recall how I ended up in my garage. Since that day, I no longer combine driving and vital calls. I follow the mindfulness principle of unitasking so I can focus 100% on driving or on calls and do a better job of each. Now one of my favorite expressions is, "Don't confuse activity with accomplishment."

My favorite recreational activity is downhill skiing because, to ski fast and safely down the mountain, I have to be focused and perfectly present in the moment. I cannot think about work or other stresses in my life while I'm planning my "line" or path down the mountain. If I'm not in the moment, I run the risk of hurting myself or others or, even worse, sustaining a mortal injury. There is plenty of time to socialize or think about other things when I'm riding the lift up the mountain.

Skiing, driving, the ringing in my ears, and conversations with other CEOs made me aware of the hazards of distracted multitasking, and I knew that something had to change in my life and at Delta Dental. Fortunately, with all of this "craziness" around me, my family, Delta Dental and in the entire business community, into my life walked Annabel Beerel, a guru of mindfulness. As you will read, her training has made a huge difference for Delta Dental and our employees.

At Delta Dental, we have used a continuing series of in-house seminars by Annabel, plus many articles and guided meditation to put mindfulness into practice. We have learned that mindfulness is not just the latest "buzzword" in business. It is life changing when practiced authentically and regularly.

Here's what one of our employees said after participating in the mindfulness series.

"We have a great culture here at Delta Dental. I'm so grateful to Tom Raffio for providing this mindfulness training. When I got the announcement about the seminar series I thought, 'What a great thing for a company to do.' It convinces me this is the right place to be."

A final thought for leaders like me who want to introduce mindfulness to your organizations and for anyone who wants to learn and practice mindfulness. Mindfulness does not happen in an hour. It takes work and dedication. The foundation of mindfulness is meditation. Meditation and mindfulness both have to be learned and practiced. They are easy, natural, and enjoyable once we learn them. Like all worthwhile things, we have to stick to them to get the most from them.

I know you will find this book helpful as you thoughtfully alter your life's habits. I know this book will help you liberate yourself from frustrating and unproductive routines and become a better family member, employee, manager, and human being.

MINDFULNESS AT WORK

This book is primarily aimed at business leaders and managers. It concerns mindfulness at work.

In the ensuing chapters, we explain what mindfulness is and the role of meditation in building our mindfulness capacities. We explain how mindfulness brings us to greater wholeness, to a greater sense of self, and to a greater personal empowerment. By practicing mindfulness, we are healthier, we think better, we relate better, and we perform better. Mindfulness helps us to be more integrated, more embodied, and more present to everything we do.

Mindfulness is about valuing ourselves and valuing others. It is about making every moment count, because only the present moment exists. Mindfulness encourages us to give our special attention to every moment, as every moment holds untold lessons and untold opportunities, if we can just see them.

Mindfulness builds our self-awareness and strengthens our self-mastery. These two together feed our sense of self-worth in a way that no external agent can.

Mindfulness is about personal transformation. It is about being different. It is about seeing differently. It is about embracing life and the world with greater openness, acceptance, and appreciation.

The inner strength that mindfulness provides helps us be more adaptive, more thoughtful, more creative, and more self-contained. It provides us access to our inner center, our anchor, in this topsy-turvy world. It also helps us to think more clearly amidst the myriad distraction of daily life, to focus, and to perform more effectively.

Our book is full of stories of how mindfulness and meditation have impacted people at the personal level and professionally. It has improved their lives, their relations, and their ability to perform. It has helped them grow and become more open to change.

We encourage you to bring mindfulness into your culture. You will find mindfulness is the most powerful tool you have. As you will see through the stories we relate, mindfulness makes for a better me, a better you, a better world.

Chapter 1

A Topsy-Turvy World

THINGS FALL APART

"Things fall apart; the centre cannot hold;
mere anarchy is loosed upon the world."
– William Butler Yeats

So it seems for many of us. We live in a topsy-turvy world. Things are out of balance. Everything is changing at once and there is no center, no anchor point, certainly not outside of oneself.

Challenges in every domain continue to mount. Home life is filled with all kinds of pressure and stresses. College kids, mounting college fees, aging parents, and skyrocketing healthcare costs are just a few of the many trials facing many Americans.

Organizational life is precarious. Pressure at work has increased. Layoffs continue; downsizing continues; outsourcing continues. The social and political spheres are also besieged from every possible direction. Both international and domestic turmoil is infused with new shades of violence, adding a further layer of anxiety to an already anxious, stressed, and over-taxed populous.

An added, deeply-rooted concern, is that our nation's health is at risk. Close to fifty percent of the population now suffers from chronic diseases, and the numbers are mounting. Stress may be the root cause of, or at least a contributor to, many of these illnesses. And, as I see it, external stressors are not going away.

A final comment about our topsy-turvy world is that I think we are misusing our minds. We have become shackled to round-the-clock media and digital distractions that are ruining both our minds and our relationships. We are rarely present to ourselves, let alone anyone else. Our addiction to multitasking, to the deafening noise of our technological wonders, and to the use of gadgets for everything short of eating and sleeping, is taking the humanity out of everything we do. The dissonance between our true inner needs and our daily actions is, I believe, adding to our distress and dis-ease.

FROM THE CEO's DESK

As a CEO of a medium-sized organization, Northeast Delta Dental (Delta Dental), well positioned in the dental insurance field in New England, I am looking at the corporate landscape with some dismay. We truly live in a topsy-turvy world. The competing claims to build a sustainable business, create a healthy and adaptive culture, and be a good corporate citizen seem intractable.

There is no question we are facing not just one, but many paradigm shifts. The time when corporations identified with a certain industry, fought for their corner of the market, and played to certain rules, is long gone. Now, everything is up for grabs as the large players, with massive market power and distribution networks, extend their tentacles into every corner of every industry.

THE "COMMODITIZATION" OF AMERICA

I frequently talk about the commoditization of America, what I mean by this is, businesses are "racing to the bottom" to make goods and services less expensive to produce and market, eventually passing this savings along to the consumer. Consumers expect everything to be easily accessible at the lowest price. As a result, everything is being turned into a commodity. By massive scaling in production and distribution, economies of scale allow for a drastic reduction in prices. This of course leads to the pressure to sell ever higher volumes to generate adequate profits. This also means that demand is no longer the problem. The problem now is how to get rid of oversupply which is why we rush to Africa and India where we happily dump our excess goods.

To overcome the volume-oversupply challenge, the "big box" stores are forced to find new industries and new markets in which they can continue to build volume. Business has become a never-ending search into how to penetrate existing markets, or find new ones, at any price. Massive volumes marketed at massively reduced prices is the name of the game.

THE DISRUPTION OF INDUSTRIES

The commoditizing trend, and the hunt for volume and market share, along with the development of technology and the internet, has spurred on the disruption and erosion of industry boundaries. As I see it, there is no longer a clear definition of an industry. The boundaries are increasingly blurred. One can no longer say these types of companies provide these types of products and services. One can also no longer say that to procure this type of product or service one needs to visit such and such a company or store.

Boundaries are also blurred by our outsourcing trend and by the growing entry of foreign companies into the domestic market. Again, I am not saying this is a bad thing. I am a supporter of international trade and of open and fair trade agreements. What I am seeing is that the commoditizing trend is magnified and accelerated as large overseas companies hunt for volume too. One example is how a traditional auto company is building robots for the medical field and developing automated prostheses for people who are paralyzed. It is just one jump of the imagination to speculate that Toyota will soon build semi-automated hospitals.

Many "big box" stores, having expanded geographically, have expanded product offerings, adding groceries, pharmacy services, and even minute clinics. Can it be long before these companies enter the insurance or hospitality industries? These companies have the reach, the brand image, the logistical capability, and most importantly the financial muscle. There is no end to anything!

THE INTERNET MENTALITY

Another key feature of this topsy-turvy, changing world of ours is the growing internet mentality. This has had an enormous impact on industries, way more than any of us would have ever imagined.

For one, all companies are now becoming software driven. In the old days, computers were used essentially for administrative, accounting, and some basic marketing and inventory management functions. Increasingly now, many products and services are essentially embedded in software. A prime example is books or videos. Software is part of the product or service. This has arisen because of the huge shift in the method of distribution. Distribution is now driven by the internet. There is almost nothing one cannot buy online. And, more and more, there is nothing one cannot download online, other than of course tangible products.

The service economy we have become is driven by the internet. For us at Delta Dental, many years ago we used computers in the standard back-office fashion. Now, much of our business is centered on our software systems. It networks our providers, our customers, our insurance relationships, our risk management systems—you name it. We deliver our insurance over the internet. We have become a software company that focuses on oral health as opposed to a dental benefits company that uses technology to service its customers and dentists. I doubt if there are many other organizations that provide services that have not faced this same shift.

There is one other aspect of the internet that is, of course, relevant—it heightens the transparency between goods and services. In other words, it makes it easier and faster for people to compare value-for-price for what is on offer. This increases competition, which we know, also drives down prices. So, the internet is a key factor in the volume-price-commoditization trend.

PEOPLE

The trends I describe place a lot of pressure on people. At home, we may all benefit from cheaper services or gadgets, but there is a price to pay. At work the organization must provide more for less. This has an impact on employees as more is expected of them. They need to be more productive, more efficient, and more accountable. The organization's profits and cash flows are squeezed and so there is no spare capital to cater for spare human capacity. Everyone must perform to the maximum. We feel short-staffed. CEOs of other organizations I speak to experience the same dynamic.

In this topsy-turvy changing world, we are also continually investing in new initiatives. We have several change projects on the go at any one point in time. Our people are expected to treat change as normal. While we provide every support and every training we can, we also expect our employees to adapt and learn quickly and efficiently. This places them under a lot of stress. All the parts are moving all the time. There is little or no room for rest and reflection before the next change happens again. Speaking with other business leaders and managers, they talk about the same challenges. It is all go, go, adapt, change, rework, rescale, restructure—endlessly.

This intense pressure felt by everyone fuels multitasking. But multitasking is a misnomer. We stress ourselves by trying to do too much at once and delude ourselves by thinking we are accomplishing more.

As I mentioned earlier, people are stressed at home and stressed at work. And these stresses tumble into one another. People go home stressed and arrive at work stressed. Amidst all this, we are asking them for peak performance. How can the center hold?

THE BOTTOM LINE

All existing business models are radically under siege. The way we used to make money, or generate a positive bottom line, is very different to the way we do now. What used to be cost centers are now direct costs and vice versa. The emphasis of operations has shifted. Distribution has become a major driving force in business.

Not only has the cost structure of our business changed, but we too are stressed to chase volume. While our industry is still regulated, and is thus not totally prey to free market forces, this is changing. I anticipate that soon we will see some significant changes in the industry margins here too and new entrants to our space. No organization is impervious to the trends I have described. So — what can one do?

A GOOD CORPORATE CITIZEN

Despite these changing trends, we at Delta Dental remain committed to being good corporate citizens. What that means for us, is that we care about the culture of the organization. Communication, teamwork, quality, and integrity are our core values. We strive to live those values in everything we do.

Employees have a community at Delta Dental. We host many events and recognition ceremonies to show the respect and value we have for our people. We are committed to personal and professional development, and invest significantly in programs that advance employees' talents, skills and well-being. We support our local community by funding events, attending events, and sponsoring our employees who volunteer and participate in non-profit organizations.

Maintaining this commitment is not easy amidst the stresses of time and mental capacity mentioned above. I am not sure how to keep it all going. My team feels the same way. Something must give — but what? Everything is important and urgent and needed. How does one find one's center amidst it all?

MINDFULNESS AT NORTHEAST DELTA DENTAL

In pondering these matters, we decided at Delta Dental to implement a program on mindfulness. We began this program in the first quarter of 2017, and it is going strong. The benefits are beyond what I expected, especially within such a short space of time. In the chapters that follow, we share some of Delta Dental's experiences in implementing this program.

We are not saying that mindfulness is a panacea. Panaceas do not exist. What we have found is that mindfulness and meditation help people find that inner anchor. It gives them a place of inner poise and calm that helps them deal with some of the stresses and strains of this topsy-turvy world. As you will see, some of the stories are remarkable.

Chapter 2

This Thing Called Mindfulness: What It Is and How We Practice It

ENCOUNTER IN BANGKOK

It was 1986. Those were the good old days. I was flying from London to Bangkok en route to Singapore. Despite the fifteen-hour flight, flying was an adventure. There was no disrobing at security in those days. The pilots talked with passengers in those days. The flight attendants smiled in those days. People were relaxed and excited in those days. The beverage cart, full of all kinds of intoxicating delights, would rumble up and down the aisle where eager hands received an unending supply of free samples. Those were the good old days!

On landing in Bangkok, the Jumbo 747 disgorged its weary passengers onto a sizzling tarmac. Following the others, I stumbled down the steps into another world. Looking around, I was certain I had landed on a strange planet. Everything, and I mean *everything*, was different. The sky, the people, the smells, the noises, the buildings, the language, the food—everything!

Having fought my way through customs and the baggage claim, I managed to find the taxi rank. This was no mean task. Everything was written in Thai. English signs were few and far between.

The airport was jam-packed with what seemed to be millions of people mingling throughout the terminals eager to sell you something—a flower, a fruit, a lottery ticket, or a rickshaw ride.

Safely in the taxi, I began to inspect this other world. Besides the bedlam of the roads, filled with rickshaws, donkeys, elephants, bicycles, broken-down vans, trucks, and smoke-belching buses, the mass of movement was astounding. As we crawled through the traffic-jammed streets, I was struck by the myriad shrines, temples, and stupas that defiantly declared their presence amidst the rest of the seething cacophony. On every corner, there was a prayer stand. Ochre-garbed monks walked peacefully amidst the moving masses, appearing and disappearing as we wound our way to my hotel.

My visit to Bangkok was one of those "spots in time" that changes one's life. I had many adventures on that visit, including rescuing a nun who had fallen off the ferry into the Chao Phraya River, the main waterway that runs through the city. One of the significant memories of that trip was my encounter with an old Buddhist monk.

On the second day, I decided to devote some time to exploring the magnificent temples and shrines. I visited several, taking off my shoes, and sitting quietly on one of the many mats before an incense-filled altar boasting a statue of some manifestation of the great Buddha. I noticed that as one stepped out of the frenetic chaos of the Bangkok streets into any temple or shrine, the atmosphere of peace and harmony was soul-refreshing. It presented an indescribable contrast to the outside world. It was as if one had stepped into a little piece of heaven.

At my last temple of the day, I attempted to engage with some of the monks tending the altars. We made scant progress as their English was minimal, and my Thai non-existent. An older monk who seemed in charge, walked slowly towards me. He spoke excellent English. In hushed tones, we had a brief and superficial discussion about Buddhism and its devotion to peace and serenity. I commented on the marvelous quiet and stillness within the temple as compared with the streets outside. The old monk responded: "What you are noticing in the streets is what goes on in your own mind. Buddhist meditation is finding the temple inside the mind. We are so busy living in the outside streets, that we do not realize the peace and harmony is accessible to all of us within. We have to step inside our own temple."

From that moment, that day, I vowed to learn about the temple of the mind. So began my journey into the world of comparative religions and cultures.

HABITS OF MIND

In 1986, I was deeply steeped in developing my AI systems. I spent hours every day with experts in various domains, learning about their expertise and their decision-making paradigms. I read everything I could about the mechanics of the mind. I also spoke with many so-called decision-making experts. All of us marveled at the capacity of the human brain. Many were caught up in the hubris that we can capture the mind and capture its workings in some machine. I am sure God must be laughing!

Despite my in-depth investigations, it was only when I began my own mindfulness and meditation practice that I really got an inkling of the infinite capacities of our minds. It was also then that I truly learned how I apply my mind to daily living. Boy, was that a wake-up call! Since then, I have come to learn how the distortions of my mind limit my freedom, push me into unnecessary anxiety, and prevent me from living the fullness of my life.

We all begin life with a wide-open mind that is present and accepting of everything. As we grow up and mature, due to personal and social pressures, we condition our minds. As a result, we select what we value, what we should think, what biases and prejudices suit us, and how we should behave. We also develop more and more ingrained habits of mind that keep us on automatic pilot—researchers say—over 85% of the time. In other words, we live in continuous stimulus-response where we respond out of our reservoir of ingrained reactions without even thinking. Over the years, we become less and less present to the present. We move through life in a blur of unconscious reactions with only scattered moments of truly conscious participation. Instead of freely choosing from our inner being, we act out of our storehouse of repertoires. As we discuss in these next pages, these habits of mind do not serve us well. As I have learned, they rob us of our lives!

The new interest in mindfulness, is our attempt at reversing some of these reactive and habitual behaviors that limit our freedom and feed the frenzy of daily living.

THE MINDFULNESS BUZZ

Mindfulness is the new yoga. It is another method of finding union — or yoga — with our innermost self. Mindfulness, along with its partner, meditation, helps us find the peace and relaxation that yoga also offers. In fact, in the East, the two — yoga and mindfulness — have never been separated. They are taught and practiced as one integral method of personal inner development. Together they help us discover our own inner shrine or inner sanctuary.

Years ago, people who engaged in yoga were considered a little "out there." Now the "out there" is everywhere. Yoga has become mainstream. It is no longer just for the aesthete or the eccentric — it is for everyone.

Mindfulness is following a similar path. In the 1970s, experiments in the United States using mindfulness and meditation to help with chronic diseases began to emerge as a viable medical option. The Mindfulness-Based Stress Reduction (MBSR) program initiated by Jon Kabat-Zinn in 1979, placed mindfulness and meditation squarely in the alternative health care domain.

The growth in recent years in the practice of mindfulness has been astounding. More and more individuals and organizations are embracing mindfulness as part of daily living. Some statistics report that between 15%-20% of companies are introducing mindfulness into their organizations. The reason behind this growth is that mindfulness provides a powerful antidote to the anxiety, stress, and disharmony that many contend to be their daily burden. As we discuss in the ensuing chapters, chronic illness is on the increase, as are mental disease and suicides. We are a nation in distress. Finding the inner sanctuary of our minds is a powerful method for gaining tranquility and equanimity amidst the frenetic, anxiety-driven streets of our topsy-turvy world.

In my mindfulness journey of the past thirty years, I have come to learn there is no philosophy, religion, or culture that does not have some form of mindfulness and meditation as part of its tradition. How have we forgotten this practice as part of our heritage? How have we let this jewel of inner strength get buried under the technical materialism that dominates our world? I suggest that we have been too busy in the bedlam of the streets, fighting our way to get ahead to remember that our inner sanctuary provides us with all the resources we need. Well, the time has come.

WHAT IS MINDFULNESS EXACTLY?

In this chapter, I go to some depth in explaining what mindfulness is. I could take the short cut, which many people do, and say that mindfulness is simply paying attention in the present moment with non-judgment. By short-changing the definition, I believe we miss some of the depths of true mindfulness and therefore we are less likely to experience all its benefits. Mindfulness is also not about short-cuts!

Mindfulness is a specific type of attention, not any old attention. It is an exquisite attentiveness that requires practice and refinement. It also a form of disciplined attention that is inspired by a certain motivation. That motivation is to be mindful and attentive for its own sake. We are interested in being mindful because it will bring out the best in us, not because we can use it to manipulate some other outcome.

Unfortunately, as I am sure you have noticed, we are assailed by articles, courses, and seminars, all promising us the pot of gold at the end of the mindfulness rainbow. It is our nature, it seems, to create fads propped up by all kinds of hoped for promises. In this case we have all manner of enticements to practice mindfulness to change our brains, to reduce stress, to get fit, to improve our memory, to lose weight, to think better and faster, to improve our emotional intelligence (EI), enhance our I.Q. ... you name it! Mindfulness is now hailed as the new elixir to life, aging, relationships, and happiness! While many of these promises might be realized with devoted practice, one will always get the most out of something by doing it for its own sake—for the love of doing it.

I encourage you to approach the work of mindfulness with only one enticement: it will make a better you, a kinder you, a more compassionate you, and a far more effective you. As a result, you will feel better about yourself, have better relationships, and you will make better contributions that make for a better world. Embark on the road of mindfulness *for the love of it*. The more you love it, the more it will become part of you. The results will be indescribable.

UNDERSTANDING MINDFULNESS

A Mindfulness Definition
Here is a definition I think best describes the mindfulness concept and its practice:

➜   *Mindfulness is the intentional directing of awareness to attending to the present moment, in a focused and sustained manner, with non-judgment.*

Let us work through the parts of this definition, and review the importance of each component.

MindFULNESS—The Goal
First, consider the word mindfulness. What do we want the mind to be full of? What is this "fulness" about?

If we think about the term "fulness" as in carefulness, thoughtfulness, and helpfulness, as opposed to carelessness, thoughtlessness, and helplessness, we note that we are talking about a capacity, a way of acting to the maximum, stretching to the full extent.

Mindfulness is therefore about optimizing or maximizing the capacities of the mind. To be mindful thus means to put the mind to its optimal use. If I am saying I am being mindful, I am saying

I am using my mind in the best way possible.

The best way possible is:

To use my awareness and attention to apprehend reality as it is, and to develop myself—mind, body and soul—to my utmost potential in every moment of my life.

In short: *To live life in the most aware, intentional, and engaged way that I can.*

This is the goal of mindfulness. I am going to use my mind very intentionally, as my most strategic resource, to live a fully engaged life. As we will see, a fully engaged life is one where I can alternate between the bedlam of the external world and the peace found in the inner world, with a special type of balance and equanimity. I am also going to find a new freedom in making my choices.

KEY COMPONENTS OF MINDFULNESS

Based on my definition, there are six critical components or aspects to mindfulness. These are:

1. Staying in pure awareness
2. Not making things objects
3. Attributes of attention
4. Not identifying with thoughts and feelings
5. Non-attachment
6. How we create our reality

1. Staying in Pure Awareness

Imagine you are just waking up and awareness is slowly rising out of you, like the slowly emerging sun. You smell something pleasurable, and momentarily, you open yourself to that pleasurable sensation. You experience it as it is, and appreciate it for what it is. You are enveloped by the experience. However, almost instantaneously with your experience, the conceptualizing and controlling mind jumps in and shouts "coffee, coffee!"... Bang! Your pure awareness has now been pulverized with the coffee beans into the limited world of concepts and labels. You have now "made up your mind" that your experience concerns coffee being made. The process looks something like this:

Aroma > raw sensation > sense of smell > coffee, good, thirsty, must have >>>>>>>>> split seconds

Now, let's look at what the mindful approach would be. Here we try to prolong the raw experience of something before we begin to put words to it and start labeling it. We try not to reduce what we experience by defining and limiting it. We let it be just what it is. It is like the experience of the smell of a rose before we try to describe it. It is pure, unadulterated, unprocessed, raw sensation.

The mindfulness process looks like this:

Aroma > raw sensation >>>>>>>>> sense of smell >>>>>>>>> coffee >>>>>>>>> thirsty

Note: We have slowed down the process, and eliminated judgment (good) and attachment (the "must have"). I will say more about those two later.

Part 1 of our definition states that mindfulness is a slowing down of our mind's conceptualizing process. We try to stay in the experience of something for as long as we can before we name it and isolate it out of flowing reality.

2. Not Making Things Objects

As I explained, mindfulness is our conscious striving to stay as long as we can with a sensation prior to our translating it and converting it into symbols. As soon as we name and objectify something, we lose a deep understanding of what that thing is. It sets whatever we encounter apart from us. It makes it other. It severs the interconnection among the parts of a unified whole.

In my experience, America is the greatest labeling country of all. Everyone or everything has a label. As soon as there is a group or condition wherein some commonality exists, we quickly put them, or it, in a box and give it a label. I personally have been labeled a South African, a white South African, an apartheid dissenter, a Brit, a Dutch-Brit, an Irish-South African, a white refugee, an immigrant, a resident, a non-resident, an Anglophile, and so the list goes on.

Whatever happened to just "Annabel?"

Let us go back to our coffee example: You were lying in bed delighting in, opening yourself up to, that delicious aroma that enveloped you. You and the experience were one. Then... the senses kicked in giving words—words formed by habit and conditioning. Now, that envelopment is gone—or it feels less so. It has been reduced to the concept or word of "coffee." It sits in your mind. The experience has become objectified as "coffee."

Making something "other" leads to creating something that can be labeled, used, analyzed, evaluated, or discarded. It is this defining and framing process that determines our responses to these objects.

While I was pursuing graduate studies in leadership in Cambridge, Massachusetts, one of my classmates learned that I was from South Africa. For that reason, he decided to publicly label me a racist. He made an attempt to hit me. Interestingly, although this incident was observed by nearly forty students, only a handful came to my aid. Concepts and labels frequently destroy relationships and lives.

With mindfulness, we try to objectify as little as possible. To be more realistic, we try to slow down the process that converts awareness to thoughts and words, and allow some space before the objectifying mind with all its prejudices and biases jumps in.

3. Attributes of Attention

As I mentioned earlier, mindfulness is not just any attention. It is a special type of attention that requires practice and refinement. It is a type of attention that comes from self-discipline and a genuine interest in things other than ourselves.

I have broken up attention into three component parts:

Quality of Attention

Mindfulness attention is precise, focused, and objective. It is also open, inviting, and non-judgmental. Our whole being is paying attention. We are totally present.

Have you ever walked into someone's office and asked them if they can spare a moment to discuss something, and they say "sure?" They do not lift their heads from the computer and simply continue with a "go on, I am paying attention." I don't know about you, but that response infuriates me! It is not only disrespectful in my old-fashioned book, but in no way are they really listening. They are certainly not paying attention! It would be far better if they said: "Go away, not now!"

Paying attention is more than just putting down one's pen (or computer), or listening; it is being present in a special way.

With mindful attention, one intentionally makes every effort to be open, curious, available, and non-judgmental. We try to withhold our conceptualizing and labeling mind for as long as possible. We also endeavor to limit our evaluations and judgments.

Embodied Attention

Mindful attention is also paying attention to our bodies. It is our bodies that are the instruments of experience, and it is our minds that interpret those experiences. We must remember that our minds are embodied. As the old saying goes —

A mind without a body is a ghost,
and a body without a mind is a corpse.

Since we are neither one nor the other (at this time at any rate!), we are embodied minds, or spiritualized bodies. Ignoring one or the other is like living in a haunted house.

Mindfulness is not just actions of the mind; it begins with an awareness of the body. It is the body that first experiences the raw sensations that are then communicated to our senses that almost instantaneously generate thoughts, feelings, and reactions. Our bodies are our sensors to the external world.

Being mindful therefore includes being in touch with our bodies in the present moment. For example, when we walk into that meeting, by paying attention to our bodies we notice that we are breathing in a shallow fashion. Our body is telling us something. Mindfulness is about paying attention and listening. By paying attention to our bodies, we can pick up cues far sooner than when our thoughts or reactions have kicked in. By ignoring our bodies, or being disembodied, which we often are as we live in the attic of our minds, it is too late. We have lost our "presence of mind," and probably compromised ourselves at the meeting. Perhaps... yet again.

In the Present Moment
The present moment means NOW. Not after the fact, and not before the fact, NOW.

Mindful attention is about being present to the present moment. It is not about recalling the past or anticipating the future. It is an impartial, calm, watchfulness that rests within the current reality, whatever is now... now... now. It is an awareness of life in the moments one is participating in living that life.

Paying attention in the present moment means both paying attention to the external stimuli we are experiencing, as well as attending to how we are responding to that experience. In other words, we are aware of what is occurring both outside and inside. As an event or meeting takes place, we notice the mind swiftly choosing labels, judgments, emotions, images, and impulses. Paying attention is both being aware and being self-aware simultaneously.

As you can see, mindfulness calls for an exquisitely focused attention. So, dump the idea of multitasking, or even doing two things at once! You, and I, need to engage the full capacity of our minds—our MINDFULNESS! Nothing more and nothing less.

4. Not Identifying with Our Thoughts and Feelings
One of the gifts I received from both my AI work and my studies into comparative religions is an enhanced capacity for reflection and introspection. I observed and learned the power of engaging my

awareness to become aware of itself. I marveled at how the mind can double up and observe its experiences. It can experience sensations, feelings, and thoughts, and then think about them and choose how to react to them. It is like a mirror looking at itself!

Let us take an example:

Imagine you are driving to work. Thankfully, there is little traffic, and for a change, you are not in a mad hurry. You find yourself in reflective mood. Life seems reasonable today. As you reflect you say inwardly: "I wonder why I feel so relaxed this morning? It is a nice feeling. I wish every day could be like this."

Here your awareness — the "I" — is looking at the experience "feeling relaxed."

Your awareness is looking at, or reflecting on, the awareness of being relaxed. The experiencer (you) is experiencing the experience (not you). Your mind is not identifying with what is passing through. What passes through is "other." Your mind — the "I" that does the seeing, hearing, feeling, and thinking — is not the states it experiences. It is a witness to those states. This is called non-identifying.

Now a different experience occurs when you say, "I am relaxed." Here there is only the subject — "I." The "I" does not distinguish itself from the awareness or experience of being relaxed. The "I" is the experience. There is no witness. This lack of distinction is called identification.

Don't many of our days go like this?

Oh no, I am late; I am in a hurry; I am unprepared; I am overwhelmed; I am relieved; I am mad because he…; I am thankful; I am hungry; I am tired; I am thinking; I am worried; I managed; I am so glad the day is over!

What we notice here is that our feelings rapidly turn to thoughts that capture our minds. Our sensations of anxiety, anticipation, relief, hunger, and fear, take over our minds in thought-bites that can quickly ruin our day… after day… after day. We are caught up in perpetual identification with our experiences.

With mindfulness, we deliberately shift our mindset from
"I am angry,"
to
"I am experiencing angry feelings."
We strive to non-identify. This encourages us to treat our thoughts and feelings as clouds passing over the sea. Our thoughts and feelings are acknowledged and observed as they drift by. They have no hold over us. Here I get to see the anger I am experiencing is not me. It is simply a feeling or a thought. I have a choice. Do I react to the "anger cloud" or do I just let it drift by? I am free to choose. I am not my thoughts. I am not my feelings.

I am free to choose! Non-identification gives us an opportunity to choose how we wish to respond and react to life's events. This is true empowerment.

5. Non-Attachment

You may recall our earlier discussion on waking up to that smell of coffee. Many of us say: "I have to have my early morning coffee to get me going." Coffee shops are making gazillions on our attachments!

As we practice reflection and introspection—the hallmarks of mindfulness—we soon realize how many of our waking moments are devoted to trying to control people, events, or interactions. We want more of what makes us feel good. And we want less—preferably none at all—of the things we don't like or make us afraid. More or less, we are all control freaks. Our day is run by desires and aversions beginning with that first cup of coffee.

What mindfulness and meditation teach us is that our attachments and aversions are all in the mind. Mindfulness also teaches us that everything is in continuous flux and change. No matter how intensely we desire something, there is no point in being overly attached as things will change, and the object of our attachment will alter or move on. The rivers of change never cease flowing.

Through mindfulness, we also learn (as my father so aptly pointed out) that what seems terrible today is not so bad tomorrow. What seems wonderful today is different tomorrow. Everything changes. Everything passes by like the clouds. We should enjoy what we enjoy and let it go. We should not let fear immobilize us, as whatever is threatening too shall pass.

Through fewer and fewer attachments to people, things, and events, we find a new poise, a new equanimity, and a new perspective in life.

6. How We Create Our Reality

There is a well-known adage that we see the world not as it is, but as we are.

This saying reminds us that we create our reality. The world we construct for ourselves is based largely on our perceptions, biases, interpretations, judgments, superstitions and conditioned philosophies, and principles. Change these, and we change our experience of the world.

Mark Twain once said: "I am an old man and have known a great many troubles, but most of them never happened."

How many of us cannot resonate with that?

As I mentioned earlier, we experience reality through our conscious perceptions and interpretations in "thought-bites." As we experience the world, through perception, thoughts, labels, words, and feelings, we dilute, disintegrate and fragment the fullness of reality. We are also deeply attached to our snatched pieces, frequently forgetting that they are just fragments of reality and do not give us the whole interrelated picture. The concepts, symbols, ideas, and images which we construct and rely on, are not the real thing. They are one sliver, one slice, one biased, myopic peep at the whole. This does not make our reality worthless, just very limited. And of course, we cannot go around punching people based on our reality. Yet we do!

Mindfulness slows down the snatching, the identifying, and the analyzing. It opens up space for wider perspectives, challenging alternatives and creative new options. Mindfulness gets us to change our spectacles and our viewing points from time to time, and to see and appreciate other realities, other possibilities, other interpretations.

Who gains with just one bit more mindfulness? You, your relationships, your organization, and the whole world.

In the next chapter, we discuss how.

MINDFULNESS—HOW WE PRACTICE IT

People frequently ask how one practices mindfulness. They say now that they know what it is, they want handbooks on how to apply it.

Mindfulness is really very simple. The "what" is also the "how." Pay exquisite attention, non-judgmentally, now to whatever you are doing. Being mindful is the doing of mindfulness. There is no separation. You are mindful when you listen, talk, email, go to a meeting, and execute your tasks. In essence:

- We are present to the present moment. We bracket off the past and the future
- We experience with both our minds and our bodies
- We are attentive to what we are experiencing as we experience it
- We experience without words and pay attention without judgment
- We do not identify with people or events
- We are open to whatever we are encountering and appreciate the potential it brings
- We practice meditation

SIMPLE MINDFULNESS: A PLACE TO BEGIN

- Slow down whenever you can
- Talk less
- Listen more
- Reduce multitasking
- Notice your breath—engage in breathing exercises regularly
- Use time alone for quietness and stillness
- Turn off the cell-phone, radio, TV

- When you eat, eat. When you walk, walk. When you attend, attend
- Listen with mindfulness
- Speak with mindfulness
- Meet with mindfulness
- Engage daily in some specific ritual with mindfulness.
- Focus on the gratitude of each day
- Have some meaningful images in your office and special rooms of your home that remind you to stay in the present

Chapter 3

The Benefits of Mindfulness

BLACK MONDAY

It was 1987. The world was changing in dramatic ways. Living in London at the time, I was continually reminded to be on the alert for abandoned parcels and bags that might carry IRA bombs. Soccer hooliganism was killing people. International hostage-taking dominated the news. Tension in the Middle East was growing. The world was changing.

At the time, I was running my small and growing AI business. Things were going well, and I believed we were on a straight run to growth and prosperity. Then, Black Monday! The stock markets of the world plummeted. Billions of pounds were wiped off the stock market scorecards. London's financial center, known as the City, was in chaos. The media went berserk, and the markets plummeted some more. Within one day, five of my clients—mostly financial organizations—canceled or postponed their orders. The intense pressure to fill the sales pipeline began.

The following months were very, very difficult. Cash flow was tight. New orders were few, small, and far between. Clients paid late. Some of our competitors closed shop and technology share prices plunged. I worked around the clock trying every trick I knew to shore up business and keep the cash flow coming in. My bankers hounded me. I was exhausted, anxious, aggravated, and grouchy. How could this happen? We were doing so well, and now our prospects were snatched from us. Amidst my fretting, I heard my father's voice. "It is no good getting mad. Change your mind. Take every day at a time and work with the challenges of the day. Everything shall pass. You can handle it. Stay centered."

One Saturday afternoon, sorely in need of some downtime and some perspective, I took myself off to one of my favorite haunts at Covent Garden. I parked myself at one of the outside tables, and ordered a beaker of French champagne. I settled back and listened to the music of a trio of female violinists. While I was simply resting, enjoying being present and in the moment, a young man sat down at my table. I noticed he was carrying the *Tao Te Ching*—the Chinese classical text—which he placed on the table next to me. We smiled at one another and then turned to the musicians.

After some time, the young man rose to leave. As he did so, he turned to me and smiled saying: "The book is for you. It will help you." With that he pressed the book in my hand and left. You can imagine my astonishment. I opened the book on the page where he had a bookmark and read:

> *"She who is centered in the Tao*
> *Can go where she wishes, without danger.*
> *She perceives the universal harmony,*
> *even amid great pain,*
> *because she has found peace in her heart."*

Dumbfounded, I was reminded yet again that perspective, strength, courage, and deep resources reside within. In topsy-turvy times, one needs to anchor oneself inside oneself. My mindful moments had opened me up to an unexpected opportunity and this poignant reminder.

Singing, I strode back over Waterloo Bridge to collect my car and head home. Waiting for me was a message on my answering machine from a Sheik in Saudi Arabia. He was placing an order for twelve expert systems. He needed them urgently.

THE GOAL OF MINDFULNESS

In Chapter 1, I presented the goal of mindfulness as:

To use our awareness and attention to apprehend reality as it is, and to develop ourselves — mind, body, and soul — to our utmost potential in every moment of life.

In short: *To live a life in the most aware, intentional, and engaged way that one can.*

Many might say they are living an aware, intentional, and engaged life. They do not need all this reflection and introspection. Things are simply going fine.

I hope that this and the following chapters will encourage you to try some intentional mindfulness. You will see that the power of slowing down — something so contrary to our normal reactions — will give you a new freedom, greater perspective, and more poise and equanimity. And no, you do not need beakers of French champagne or Sheiks to bail you out. Mindfulness will help you find the resources within.

THE BENEFITS OF MINDFULNESS — A SNAPSHOT

Here are some of the important benefits of mindfulness. We expand on these in the discussion that follows, and then sum up in a more detailed manner.

- Mindfulness helps us slow down the conceptualizing and judging mind as we pay attention to the present moment
- Mindfulness sets the agenda for our wandering attention
- Mindfulness encourages us to be more present to the present
- When we are mindful, we are more attuned to reality as our conditional thinking is diffused
- We manage our perceptions more thoughtfully and less fearfully
- Mindfulness slows down our reactive behaviors
- We have more time and greater freedom to choose

- In general, the slowing down process of mindfulness is greatly stress-reducing

Let us see how these benefits are attained.

SLOWING DOWN THE CONCEPTUALIZING MIND

In the previous chapter, I described how mindful awareness is a pre-conceptual knowing. I also mentioned that it is challenging to remain in that state, and usually the best we can do is to slow down the conceptualizing process.

In the hurly-burly world of daily work and activity, we invariably are forced to deal with concepts. One of the reasons a vacation is so restful and enjoyable is that our conceptualizing process is automatically slowed down as we relax. Conceptualizing takes a lot of energy.

Imagine the following:

You are lying on that sun-soaked beach, feeling the warmth, smelling the sea, listening to the gulls and the delightful laughter of children playing in the sand. As you are gently relaxing, you do not think "beach, warm, seagulls, laughter." It all melds into one glorious experience in which you are immersed and where you feel a sense of well-being. You are not anxious or afraid. From time to time, your attention pulls you from your awareness and you do think "sea or gulls or I am hungry." But for longer periods than usual, you drift in pre-conceptual awareness. How restful. How spacious and accepting you feel.

A gift of this experience is that you are present. You are in the now moment. You have bracketed off the irritations of yesterday and the anxieties of tomorrow. You are simply luxuriating in the moment.

The key question you ask yourself is: How can you bring just a smidgen of that feeling back to work and to daily life?

The mindful answer is: By slowing down the conceptualizing and judging mind as you pay attention to the present moment.

SETTING THE AGENDA FOR ATTENTION

Being Present to the Present

The life of the mind is a continuous interplay between awareness and attention.

Awareness is our conscious knowing of things. For example, we know that we are alive. We know that we know, think, and feel. We even know that we know that we are aware. Attention, on the other hand, is a focused awareness on a specific subject matter.

For example:

I am sitting at my desk writing. Suddenly out of my peripheral awareness, the smell of smoke emerges. My survival instinct says — check it out, check it out! I switch my attention from writing to checking out the smell.

Throughout my waking hours, my attention switches continuously, guided by my awareness. Awareness and attention work hand-in-hand.

Awareness is the larger consciousness, and attention is what I focus my awareness on. Where there is a lack of a specific thing on which to focus, our wandering attention creates all kinds of drama. Our self-directed attention is undisciplined and managed by our self-referential ego. This self-referential ego feeds the mind with things to worry about — notably the regrets of yesterday and the anxieties of tomorrow. This leaves us in the familiar daily position of worrying about what we did not do, and worrying about what we need to do.

Mindfulness ensures that our attention is always directed. This direction means focusing on the present moment, paying attention to what is going on right now. It is not about ruminating over the past or anticipating the future. It is about being present to the present.

Mindfulness is our internal teacher saying: "Pay attention, now!"

GRASPING REALITY

In Chapter 1, we discussed the challenges of engaging in a realistic reality that is not skewed and twisted by our conditioned mind filled with its biases and prejudices.

In my definition of the goal of mindfulness I used the term "apprehend." To apprehend means to perceive or to understand. However, apprehending has a different quality to it than the usual perceiving or understanding. There is a directness, an immediacy, in apprehending. When we apprehend something, we grasp it intuitively as well as cognitively. It is the experience of seeing or grasping something in a flash. We just get it.

This kind of apprehension is a way of seeing and understanding reality. It is beyond just intellectual knowing. It is a deep and swift realization of what is true, what is real. We bypass our conditioned minds and open ourselves to grasping things at a deeper level. Mindfulness gives us those wonderful "aha" moments. We experience wonderful moments like this when we are truly present and when we are tuned in.

At Covent Garden, that afternoon, when I read the extract from the *Tao Te Ching*—I got the message in a flash. It was not just an intellectual understanding, it was something deeper than that which is hard to explain. It can only be experienced.

MANAGING OUR PERCEPTIONS

It is Friday at 10 am. You are hard at work at your desk. Suddenly your manager is standing in front of you. He asks whether you might stay an extra few minutes after work. He does not dally but moves on quickly. Your heart begins to race. Oh, no! What could this be about? He looked stressed. He did not look you in the eye. He seemed nervous.

You think back. What have I done wrong? You know you botched the proposal last week where you made an error which he thankfully caught in time. It could have cost the company a few thousand dollars. He did not seem that upset then... but maybe he was hiding it. Then you missed his lunchtime birthday party on Wednesday. You had forgotten about it and went to pick up your son from school as he was not feeling well. Everyone had asked where you were. So your absence was conspicuous.

And now this morning, at the early Friday meeting, you had voiced disapproval with one of his new policy suggestions. Oh no! This does not augur well. Why does he want you to stay behind when everyone else has gone? Will he fire you? Write you up? Demote you? Oh no! How will you concentrate and get through the day?

What you do not know is that your manager is anxious because he needs to take a sudden leave of absence to take care of his dying mother. He needs someone strong to take his place. Someone who is not afraid to stand up to others and disagree. Someone who has the right priorities by taking care of her son. Someone human, who is not perfect and can make mistakes and learn from them. He is feeling bad about having to do this and about having to ask you to step in at short notice.

Instead you have driven yourself to distraction. Something inside you is shouting "oh no! Survival is at stake." Your mind has moved into fear, anxiety and self-criticism. You have imagined all the "bad" things that happened and how they are resulting in bad karma. Your tendency to identify with everything as being about you has made the whole saga about you. Your blood pressure went up. Your hands began to sweat and concentration for the day went out the window. Not long thereafter, you had a tension headache and could not eat lunch. Worse still, all the "what if" scenarios kicked in. What if...

THE SAVING POWER OF MINDFULNESS

The obvious and important point here is that the perceptions we feed our brains radically influence the realities we experience. This is where mindfulness plays a hugely important role. Mindfulness slows down the conceptualizing and perceiving process. We work on not immediately jumping to our default positions, our conditioning, our negativities, our frightened egos. We slow down to get perspective. We try not to identify with our emotions. We do not dwell on what could happen. We stay in the present, in the now moment, and let the day take care of itself. We breathe and let our bodies calm down. And deeply we know that nothing can ever harm us if we do not give it the power. That is the freedom of choice we experience. That is the power of mindfulness.

(In Chapter 4, The Mind and The Brain, we explain the neuroscience finding of our reactions.)

DEVELOPING OURSELVES

Mindfulness is about self-development. It increases our cognitive, emotional, physical, and spiritual capacities and maturities. It is an act of personal transformation. Through this personal transformation, we transition into ever new levels of potential. The more we develop and invest in our potential, the more human we become.

With mindfulness, we shift our conditioned, reactive, habitual frames of reference, biases, and prejudices to be more open and less judgmental. Mindfulness also develops our capacity for empathy, compassion, and loving kindness. (We explain this further in the next chapter on meditation.)

All in all, with mindfulness there is a gentling of the world. The sharp edges of the conceptual life are softened and rounded, and the spirit of life can more easily flow through its structures.

THE BENEFITS — SUMMING UP

- We slow down the racing, jumping, undisciplined mind
- We eliminate — as much as we can — judgment and attachment
- Our attention is focused, stable, and present
- We are more self-aware
- We are in greater attunement with our bodies
- We live in the present moment in an intentional, engaged way
- We do not identify with our thoughts or feelings, so we are less emotionally charged
- We are less compulsive and driven by our habitual patterns of behavior
- We experience personal transformation in self-understanding and outlook

- The reality we create for ourselves is not as constricting as before
- We are present to the present
- We have greater freedom to choose

In Chapters 6-11, you will also read how the benefits cited above directly impact our lives and our world at work.

WHAT'S THE CATCH?

This mindfulness business sounds too good to be true! What's the catch?

The catch, as always, is in the mind.

If you wish to be freer, calmer, more present, more engaged, and more alive, there is no catch. There is, however, some work to do. If, on the other hand, you have no desire to be freer, or calmer, or more engaged, then you might say there is a catch. It all depends on your state of mind.

THE WORK OF MINDFULNESS

Developing mindfulness requires some work. I have listed this work under the following categories:

- Self-mastery
- Willpower and intention
- Perseverance
- Patience
- Managing the ego
- Focus and concentration
- The mindfulness commitment

SELF-MASTERY

Mindfulness is a form of self-mastery. Self-mastery is our ability to control our actions, impulses, and emotions. It is our conscious self-regulation through observance and reflection. We need self-mastery to grow up, develop and progress.

Self-mastery depends on two factors: self-awareness and self-discipline. Mindfulness, and its critical partner, meditation, together provide powerful methods for increasing our self-awareness and self-discipline. These two inter-dependent methods of self-inquiry and self-management depend upon the strength of our willpower and our intention.

WILLPOWER AND INTENTION

Embarking on the mindfulness path takes willpower. We do not talk (or write) much about the will, yet it lies at the very heart of who we are and how we show up in the world. It is our will that decides what does and what does not get done.

At times, our will surges through us with unbelievable strength. Without hesitation, we find the courage to fight, or stand up, or say no! At other times, our will might present itself in more subtle ways. A small voice might urge us to take a specific course of action or prompt us to do things we would not normally do. Frequently, we encounter the will when we are caught in a struggle, or when we are wrestling with some obstacle, or when we are weighing alternative courses of action. As living beings, the will gives us the power to choose and directs our choices.

With mindfulness, the choice lies in whether we commit to engaging the will to do something that may seem unfamiliar, require effort, determination, perseverance, and result in a new sense of self, or whether we choose instead to remain in the murky pond of unreflective existence. Can we commit to taking a step on the mindfulness path this moment, and then the next, and the next? Do we have the willpower to set the intention and sustain that intention?

PERSEVERANCE

In our bi-weekly mindfulness sessions at Delta Dental, we allow space for people to discuss their struggles to get their will power to engage and commit to more intentional mindful activity.

Employees talk openly about how challenging it is to be mindful in the rushed hustle and bustle of every day. They share stories about times when they can focus and be mindful, as when they are doing yoga, walking the dog, or lying on the beach.

They describe how quickly the "normal" mind (which we know is the distracted, anxious, self-serving mind), rushes in and takes over. Finding the entry point where the mind can control the mind, or where will power can insert itself, is difficult. Finding that entry point is one of the enormous benefits of meditation, something we discuss in Chapter 4.

Basically, many of us are a little lazy when it comes to persevering with less usual things like controlling our minds. Daily life has so many claims on us that one more thing just seems too much. In the case of practicing mindfulness, our will can be tempted to defer to the easy side of our nature to take control. It can favor inertia and unwillingness to take the trouble to discipline the mind. The expenditure of effort might seem too much and/or not worthwhile.

PATIENCE

With mindfulness, we are essentially changing our minds. As we discuss in the next chapter on the Mind and the Brain, we are literally changing them too. The results, however, take time to manifest themselves, and may not seem as astounding and as dashing as say managing to hit a baseball or running a marathon. Yet the longer-term impact of mindfulness is, in fact, astounding. We simply need the patience to let it show itself. And of course patience requires will power too.

MANAGING THE EGO

Our egos add to our mindfulness challenges. As we discussed earlier, unattended, unfocused, undisciplined attention is like an unruly child. It is most often referred to as the "monkey-mind," as it is continually jumping from one thing to the next like a wild monkey.

This jumping around, undisciplined attention is managed by the ego and is mostly caught up in self-referential thinking. This thinking is all about me and propping up my ego and/or making sure that I am safe and in control. It is also focused on what I should avoid and what I should attach to. I avoid what I do not like or I am afraid of, and I attach to everything that makes me feel good about myself—starting first thing in the morning with that coffee, I MUST HAVE!

No wonder we are so tired at the end of the day!

The neuroscientists refer to the self-referential tendency as the default mode network. When our minds are not focused, we default into this self-absorbed, planning and controlling mode that takes us far away from the present moment.

FOCUS AND CONCENTRATION

Mindfulness calls for focus. This is a type of attention that requires concentration. An important point here is that the focus is not forced. We are not trying to solve a complex mathematical problem. We are focusing on the present moment in a calm, alert, and sustained way. Our focus is gentle, yet alert. It arises out of our genuine interest in what is happening now... now... now.

This focus of course requires some mental effort. We do need to concentrate. However, this is not a painful exercise. This is simply taking a real interest in what the present moment holds, for it is the only reality that counts.

Setting the intention is the first step. Following through requires will power. Can you do it? Most certainly. It takes a little patience and perseverance.

How to begin. Small steps... taken for the love of it. The love of who you are and what you will become. Don't focus on the results. Find love in the experience and the results will be indescribable.

THE MINDFULNESS COMMITMENT
- To grow in self-awareness and self-discipline
- To enlist our willpower and set the intention
- To exercise perseverance and determination
- To practice focus and concentration

- To demonstrate patience
- To let what will be, be

We know from many experiences in life that what we put in determines what we get out. Is it worth it? Only you can decide whether you will invest the effort, the energy or the will power. One thing you can know for sure, this investment will not only reap huge benefits but also will pay unexpected dividends. No external factor can take your mindfulness experience away from you or diminish its meaning. Just trying with an open heart and an open mind will prove transformative. Hopefully that is return enough!

THE END OF INSOMNIA
Between sixteen and twenty-two people of Delta Dental regularly attend mindfulness sessions. These sessions last for ninety minutes. They are broken up into sections of meditation, movement and discussion.

Many of the attendees report significant changes in their ability to focus and concentrate and in their quality of attention. Some mention a greater ability to handle the stresses in home life and to be calmer and more productive at work. Several people mention that they sleep better and that their listening skills have been enhanced.

One senior executive mentions how mindfulness has totally changed her life. Since she has begun meditation, her life-long struggle with insomnia has ended. She now meditates before going to sleep, and manages to sleep through the night. She also claims that she has ceased using her anxiety medication. Every time I meet this woman, she throws her arms around me in gratitude. I am humbled as she is the one who did all the work. It was her determination and her willpower, and within three months, she is living a different life.

Another Delta Dental manager claims that mindfulness has helped her with a general social anxiety. She tends to over analyze everything before she speaks in fear of making a mistake or looking stupid. This makes it difficult for her to participate effectively in conversations.

Since she began the mindfulness sessions at Delta Dental, she has found that her anxiety has diminished and that she is finding her voice.

One customer care executive talks about how mindfulness has enabled her to be more present to customers and that she is better able to pay attention to their needs and to respond more effectively.

Several attendees speak about how their sleeping has improved, as have their relationships at home. They are more able to be present to their families, feel less stressed and feel they can manage the boundary between work and home more effectively.

LIVING WITHOUT MINDFULNESS
We experience:
- Tiredness
- Stress and anxiety
- Loss of the depth of experiences
- Poor quality of attention
- Everything is about me!
- Missing the preciousness of each moment

LIVING WITH MINDFULNESS
We experience:
- Less tiredness
- Less stress and anxiety
- Being less judgmental
- Having better management of our perceptions
- Greater presence of mind
- Greater perspective
- Greater freedom to choose

With mindfulness, we are healthier, we think better, we relate better, we perform better, we are more embodied, and more present to everything we do.

We create a better me, a better you, a better world!

Chapter 4

The Mind and The Brain

FLASHBACK

As a young girl, my Saturdays were devoted to visiting my grandmother. She lived in an apartment in the middle of Johannesburg. Prior to fleeing from Germany, she had been a concert pianist. Now, her tiny lounge was taken up with a baby grand piano my father had bought her. Without her music, she would have never survived the trauma of her escape. Music had been her life, and what kept her alive now was music.

My grandmother could play the piano beautifully. She could play any tune, without sheet notes, from Brahms to Elvis Presley. We used to have fun together. I used to sing her songs that I learned from the radio. She would play the music even though she had never heard the song. She also taught me a few melodies where I would play at one end of the piano and she at the other.

I remember one day vividly. I was ten years old. My grandmother and I had shared one of our fun mornings of music, song, and great German sausage sandwiches. After lunch, I went downstairs as usual to wait for my mother. Suddenly a motorcycle roared up onto the sidewalk in front of me. The rider, a burly man, was covered in tattoos. Waving a thick chain in my face, he called me a pretty young thing and said I was going with him whether I liked it or not. I froze.

Thankfully, out of nowhere, my mother appeared. Her energy was enough to launch a jumbo jet. No one was going to mess with her daughter! The man jumped on his bike and roared off. It took me days (in truth much longer), to shake off the experience.

For years after that episode, whenever I saw even the hint of a tattoo, my heart would throb and my palms would sweat. Intense fear would grab me. My body would react at the speed of lightning. Survival instinct would kick in. Tattoos meant danger. The simple sight of a tattoo brought up a memory, an emotion and a reaction simultaneously. For a long time, I could not bring myself to stop detesting people (no matter who they were), who displayed tattoos.

Over the years, I have trained my brain not to react and not to feel that intense fear and aversion. I have come to accept that many wonderful people, who do not wish to abduct young children, have tattoos. However, recalibrating my mind and managing my emotions around tattoos has taken time and great conscious effort. As Bessel Van der Kolk, physician and psychiatrist, points out: The body keeps score!

THE MIND IN THE BODY

In his powerful book, *The Body Keeps Score*, Van der Kolk shares his years of research into trauma and its effects on the mind and the body. What is alarming is to learn the high percentage of people in the world who have experienced trauma is some way or another.

While his book focuses mostly on intense trauma like rape and domestic violence, there are also other distressing experiences such as deep humiliation, neglectful parents, or shame about family situations. Other events that may have registered deeply are, for example, traumatic school experiences, where we were led to believe we could not do math, or we could not sing, or play sport. And then there are encounters with menacing bikers!

All of us have some version of a tattoo story. It is interesting that a tattoo is something etched in our bodies. It stands as an interesting metaphor for trauma.

What Van der Kolk points out is that "tattoo" experiences are etched in our memories. And our memories are embodied. Our bodies keep score. They do not lose track of any trauma or major experience. It is all there, deeply engraved in the mind of the body.

As we discuss in this chapter, our body keeps us alive whether we know it or not. Unfortunately, many of us are inclined to take better care of our cars than our bodies. When our body is ailing, we take "it" off to the doctor and hope he or she will fix "it" quickly without too much inconvenience. We forget that our body has its own consciousness, not to mention it carries our soul.

In those people who have suffered severe trauma, Van der Kolk notes, the parts of the brain that have evolved to monitor for danger remain over-activated. At even the slightest sign of danger, real or misperceived, an acute stress response gets triggered, accompanied by intense, unpleasant emotions and overwhelming sensations. It sounds like me and those tattoos!

Van der Kolk points out that people who have experienced trauma have evolved a refined mechanism for detecting danger. They are incredibly attuned to the subtlest emotional shifts in people around them. They are continually reading other people's friendliness or hostility based on imperceptible cues such as brow tension, lip curvature, and body angles. One of the most pernicious effects of trauma, Van der Kolk reports, is that it disrupts this ability to accurately read others, rendering the trauma survivor either less able to detect danger or more likely to misperceive danger where there is none.

Many people who have experienced trauma use drugs to help them cope. Drugs produce a calming effect and slow down the body's innate emergency response system for "fight-or-flight." As we know, many of these drugs have side effects, not to mention they can become addictive.

Van der Kolk stresses that the body has a host of innate skills that can do at least as good a job as drugs, if not better, without the side effects. He explains how we can directly train our arousal system by the way we breathe, chant, move, or enjoy music — like my grandmother. As he points out, this is well known in the East and has been practiced for eons. In our country, we call it alternative medicine!

Van der Kolk highlights that mindfulness helps us regulate our own physiology, including some of the so-called involuntary functions of the body and brain. It does this through basic activities such as breathing, moving, and touching. He especially emphasizes breathing as being a very powerful healing technique. (We discuss this in detail in the next chapter.) He also advocates any form of rhythmic body exercise such as yoga, *Tai Chi*, dancing, and drumming.

WIRED FOR SURVIVAL

Let us take a moment to understand how our survival mechanism works.

According to the neuroscientists, we are wired to be on the lookout for danger. If we think about it, it makes sense. Thousands of years ago, as animals in the wild, we had to be continuously on the lookout for danger. Danger lurked everywhere. It was better to overreact and get it wrong than be devoured by the tiger! Our basic, primitive minds were programmed with what is called a negativity bias to keep us alive. Our nervous system was primed to get us ready for fight-or-flight mode.

This negativity bias and fight-or-flight programming remains within our brains. Remember our story of Friday morning and the visit from the manager in the previous chapter. Within seconds, our negativity bias had triggered all the warning signals, and like me with the biker, survival mode kicked in.

If we have experienced trauma, or some deeply impactful events, our minds are hypervigilant, and our nervous systems are even more acutely primed for danger than normal. However, as Van der Kolk and neuroscientists point out, due to the evolution of our brains, we can moderate, manage and even change our programming thereby curbing our tendency to be in a continuous state of anxious arousal. We can calm our minds and allay our fears. We can now discern, judge, deliberate and decide on our reactions, rather than just defaulting to our animal instincts.

DRAMA QUEEN—THE WANDERING MIND

There is one more challenge we must overcome and that is our inbuilt drama queen. As we discussed in Chapter 2, a wandering mind is a drama-filled mind. When the mind is not engaged in focused attention on anything, it jumps around from topic to topic, thought to thought. The topics alternate between the past and the future. The wandering mind focuses on what is wrong or could go wrong, what might happen, how we messed up, who did not treat us well, who let us down, and how we will deal with the challenges of tomorrow. The emphasis is mostly on regret and concern about the past, and anxiety, anticipation, and how to control the future. As we will see, our drama queen mind dominates a lot of our time.

The drama queen mind is very self-centered. It is all about the ego. It centers on taking care of me with all kinds of anxiety management rationalizations.

As mentioned in Chapter 2, neuroscientists refer to the pattern of neural connections of the wandering mind as the default mode network. When our minds are in this mode, brain scans pick up signals of stress, anxiety, and anger. Since more time than we realize is taken up with our counter-productive thoughts, we are continuously in some level of chronic distress. Not to mention, the topsy-turvy world we live in adds to this dis-ease.

MINDFULNESS TO THE RESCUE

If we sum up our situation, it looks something like this:

We are wired to be negatively oriented, on the alert, looking out for danger. And danger nowadays is not just physical, but psychological, emotional and economic.

If we have experienced trauma of any kind, our brains are wired even more tightly around detecting danger signals. Hints of danger put us in fight-or-flight mode within milliseconds.

When our minds are not specifically focused, they create drama and suffering in our lives through our ruminating over the past and anxiety about the future.

Because we live so much of our waking hours sandwiched between the past and the future, we are seldom present. This means we miss out big time on what is going on in the present moment. We mishear, misunderstand, misconstrue, misperceive, and make many mistakes. Life is one big MIS!

Let us face it, this wonderful mind of ours brings with it some limitations. However, as with any disease, the antidote requires applying the toxin itself. So, we are going to manage and overcome the mind's limitations by using the mind!

Mindfulness is a powerful antidote to our anxious, hypervigilant, wandering minds.

How does it do this?

- For one, it keeps the mind staying attentive to the present moment in an alert yet calm manner. Staying in the present, we are not living in the past or in anxious anticipation of the future

- The second point is that mindfulness calms down our sympathetic nervous system — the one that activates fight-or-flight — through the slowing down process aided by measured breathing, something we discuss in the chapter on meditation

- The third, and perhaps most arresting, point is that with repeated mindfulness, our brains rewire. We create new neural pathways that bypass or side-step our ingrained negativity tracks. We actively reprogram our own brains to be more positive, less anxious, and less reactive

- Lastly, by slowing down our stimulus-response mechanisms, we give our executive brain (discussed later in this chapter) more time to intervene and assess whether the danger is real or misread

A CHAT WITH THE NEUROSCIENTISTS

Thanks to the hundreds of reports pouring out of the neuroscience laboratories, neuroscience is confirming what shamans, sages, and mystics have known for thousands of years. Mindfulness and meditation can radically restructure our brains and thereby change our minds. Let us tackle changing the brain first.

As I recounted my encounter with the tattooed biker resulted in my being "frozen." I also mentioned that for years thereafter the sight of a tattoo would throw me into a panic as if I were reliving the experience. How might one explain this response from a neuroscience point of view?

In the case of danger our nervous system prepares itself for fight-or-flight. Adrenaline is pumped into our system, our heart rate increases, and our breathing become short and fast. Our bodies are made ready to fight off our attacker or to run. In my case I had no possible chance of fighting off my attacker and any escape was blocked. I was trapped. When this occurs, the nervous system does the opposite. To preserve itself it shuts down and expends as little energy as possible. Our heart rate plunges, we can't breathe, and our stomach stops working. This is where we freeze.

Now to explain this in neuroscience language. At the slightest hint of danger perceived or real, our sympathetic nervous system sends messages through our entire nervous system shouting, "danger—all hands on deck!" The amygdala, the organ of the brain involved with our emotional responses, survival instincts, and memory, activates our reactions. Within milliseconds, our memory of previous experiences and the wiring of our brains associate the event with danger. As a result, our bodies respond with a survival instinct that is faster than lightning.

In my case, I had added tattoos to my emotional memory of danger. My brain was wired to be on the lookout for tattoos. My sympathetic nervous system would trigger the warning and the amygdala would register the emotion. The two of them, working hand in hand would result in my increased heart rate and perspiration. Danger had been sighted and to survive, my body reacted. It was one swift simultaneous movement of memory-emotion-reaction. Thinking did not have a chance!

Mindfulness can slow down and even change this sequence of reactions. Deep breathing activates the parasympathetic nervous system. This is the system that counters the sympathetic nervous system. It puts the brakes on the reactive charge to fight for one's life. It does this in two ways: One is through repeated mindfulness and meditation, we have slowed down our arousal systems. Through regular practice, we have physically rewired our brains to be less reactive. We are generally calmer; less easily triggered, and more amenable to the rationalizing process of the brain.

The second way that mindfulness helps, is through calm, deep breathing. Deep breathing decreases the activity of the amygdala, which is responsible for us getting fired up about something. Its reactions in milliseconds are fifteen times faster than thought! What neuroscience also reports, is that meditative practices shrink the physical size of the amygdala, thus reducing our levels of stress and anxiety and our reactive responses.

As we discussed in the previous chapters, the big thing about mindfulness is that it slows everything down. It gives us a larger window in which we can choose our responses to life's events.

OUR EXECUTIVE BRAINS

We often jokingly talk about our, or someone else's, gray matter. Whether we know it or not, gray matter is indeed a measure of our brain capacity. Gray matter is the colloquial term for the cerebral cortex. This is the wrinkly, outermost layer of the brain tightly packed with neurons. The thicker, and more wrinkled this gray matter, the more youthful, active, and healthy the brain. Neuroscientists report that mindfulness increases our gray matter.

The prefrontal cortex is the section of the cerebral cortex that lies at the very front of the brain just behind the eyebrows. It is often referred to as the executive brain. This part of our brain is involved in managing complex processes like reasoning, logic, problem solving, planning, and short-term memory. It is thought to play a significant part in directing attention, developing and pursuing goals, and inhibiting counterproductive impulses.

While the executive brain is from our perspective the most "powerful" function of our brain, it is one of the slowest parts of our nervous system. Thanks to our highly-developed innate survival system, our reactions are much faster than our rationalizing, executive brain. Relatively speaking, our "plodding," thinking brain needs time to catch up. Mindfulness provides that time.

SOME NEUROSCIENCE FINDINGS
Stress, anxiety, the effects of trauma, nervous disorders and chronic diseases, all benefit from mindfulness and meditation practices. Better health improves emotional stability.

- Meditators have thicker cortexes (more gray matter), which enhances the executive functions of the brain
- Mindfulness focuses the scattered energies of the mind, redirecting it to healthy living, problem solving, and inner healing
- Through meditation and mindfulness, people can create new neural paths that change associations and reduce arousal and reactivity
- Mindfulness helps us pay focused attention to our bodily sensations, thereby improving attention and presence
- People with mindful practices focus better amidst multiple distractions. The executive function of the brain has an opportunity to optimize its functioning while limiting more negative and compulsive primitive behaviors
- People with mindful practices have better short-term memory functions, can concentrate for longer periods, have more mental agility and tend to think more critically
- Mindfulness keeps attention focused on the present moment. Brain scans show that this activity fires neurons associated with happiness, purpose and self-awareness

In my experience, a very high percentage of people I have worked with, either individually or as part of an organizational initiative, claim that mindfulness practice has positive health effects within a short space of time. Of course, better health improves everything else.

THE CALMING EFFECT OF MINDFULNESS— THE EVIDENCE

Here are some stories from the Delta Dental mindfulness program participants:

"I am more effective at work because I am well-rested. Since I have been more consciously trying to be mindful, I have found that I sleep more easily."

"I have come to realize that I am frequently in fight-or-flight mode. Being mindful and practicing deep breathing has helped me enormously."

"I have been on low-grade tranquilizers for years. Since I began the mindfulness and meditation classes, I have found myself to be more relaxed, more focused, and less anxious. A few weeks ago, I gave up the tranquilizers and I have been just fine. I feel so much better without those drugs in my system."

"I am currently going through some serious personal issues at home. I have been stressed to the limit. The mindfulness and meditation sessions have been enormously helpful. I have been better able to cope and to concentrate and perform at work."

IMPORTANCE OF MEDITATION

One important matter we cannot overlook is that neuroscience reports are based mostly on the impact of meditation on the brain. As we discuss in the next chapter, meditation is the foundation on which mindful living is built. If we think we can just be mindful and skip the meditation piece because it is too challenging, we will find that our mindfulness efforts will be superficial and lack endurance. It is the exercise of meditating that develops and changes the brain.

Mindfulness then reinforces the new brain patterns that then impact our behavior and thinking.

IS THE BRAIN THE MIND?

Earlier in this chapter I mentioned that mindfulness and meditation can radically restructure our brains and thereby change our minds. We have looked at how our brains change. Now, we look at our minds. I want to begin with a caveat that, since this is an enormous and complex topic, we only cover this in the most simple and abbreviated way.

Some of us learned a little of the biology of the brain at school. Few of us have really delved into the deeper question regarding the mind, what it is and how it works. We are forgiven in that it is a very complex subject, seemingly abstract, to which no-one can really provide a definitive answer. One might then say: Why bother?

Well, our mind is our most intimate reality. It is our experience of consciousness. In a sense, it defines us as being alive. Our minds also determine what we think, how we feel, and how we behave. A little curiosity is therefore in order.

WHAT WE KNOW ABOUT THE MIND

The mind has something to do with consciousness. Many state that the mind is consciousness. We are then stuck with the question: Well, what is consciousness?

In truth, despite many speculations, we do not really know.

What we can say is that we experience the mind as an instrument of consciousness. This instrument enables us to think, and to feel. It also enables us to reflect and to be self-aware.

The mind is neither energy nor matter. It cannot be measured and it does not take up space. It is also non-local. This means that it cannot be located anywhere. The mind can also dispel the idea of time and distance. Since Einstein, scientists have endorsed the idea that nothing can travel faster than the speed of light. Yet, the mind or consciousness does. It is instantaneous. Distance as we define it, is irrelevant to the passage of the mind.

We also know that the mind, or consciousness, is the subjective, interior, personal feeling of the experience of something. The experiencing subject (you or me), experiences due to consciousness. We know, feel and sense from the inside. Consciousness refers to subjectivity. It is thought, feeling, purpose, intention, choice, value, and desire. It is sentient, subjective, and has free will.

We know that consciousness is intensely personal. My feelings, tastes and auditory experiences are not the same as yours. No outsider can step into my experience.

This is what we know — more or less! As you can see, the mind eludes precise description. To some degree, we know what it enables, and we know some of its contents. After that, we are flummoxed.

WHAT WE DON'T KNOW ABOUT THE MIND

We don't know what the mind actually is — what it is made up of. We cannot point to it, measure it, locate it, take a picture of it, or track its passage. The closest we have come is to say it is consciousness or spirit. But then, as we said before, what is consciousness or spirit?

We also do not know where consciousness comes from. We are born with it, and we lose it when we die — the lights go out! We associate it somehow with our breath. Once we stop breathing, we lose consciousness.

The added mystery of consciousness (mind), is that it somehow impacts the brain. This enigma is known in science as the "hard problem." Essentially the problem relates to explaining how something that is intangible, and has no substance, can impact and influence something that is tangible and has substance. Suffice it to say that some materialists, which include a few neuroscientists, insist that consciousness somehow emerges out of the brain. How, they have yet to explain.

We are left with this question: What is the relationship between the brain and our minds?

BRAIN AS TRANSMITTER OF THE MIND

To explain the mind/brain relationship, we can use the analogy of the brain as a transmitter of the mind, just like the radio is the transmitter of the information coming from the radio station. When the transmitter is in good working order, the transmission is well received, and the transmitter conveys the information as desired.

When the transmitter is not working, or there is some electromagnetic interference, the transmitter does not pick up the signals and cannot convey the information properly. When the transmitter is old, the frequencies are garbled and confused — a little like us!

The transmitter is of course not the radio station. Similarly, the brain is not the mind, but receives and transmits its messages. The more "in-shape" our transmitter, the more ably the mind can reveal its true nature. The more distorted our transmitter — with ignorance, bias, prejudices, and frozen conditioning — the more distorted the messages received from the mind.

Meditation rewires our transmitters so that we can remove or change old conditioning and open ourselves up to the "pure mind." Mindfulness practice reinforces new neural connections, improves our health through reduced stress, and through reduced negativity or drama queen behavior, helps us be more positive in life. In other words, mindfulness and meditation improves the reception of our transmitters.

The brain is a highly dynamic, reorganizing, adaptive system. By consciously, actively, and consistently opening ourselves up to new ideas, new images, and new experiences, we can optimize the enormous capacities of our brains. The more we develop our brains — our transmitters — the more access we have to the infinite power of the "pure mind."

THE PURE MIND — TUNING THE TRANSMITTER

Above I refer to the infinite power of the "pure mind." Different traditions refer to this differently. Different people call this "pure mind" either God, Elohim, Allah, Brahman, Buddha Mind, Universal Consciousness, Mother Nature, or The Ground. Others might refer to it as our transpersonal Self, or our deepest instinct. Whatever it is, it defies exact definition or description. All we know is that it is the source of our capacity for life and consciousness — however we define that!

As the brain changes, so does our capacity for consciousness. A healthy, vibrant, mindful brain results in greater awareness and self-awareness. We are more in tune with ourselves, with others, and with the environment. We feel better about ourselves, and we experience more joy, gratitude, compassion and love. The shamans, sages, and mystics have known this for eons. Now that the neuroscientists tell us this is so, more people believe it.

How does this work? I will do my best to explain what I understand as a result of my years of study in comparative religions and spiritual psychology.

Staying with our analogy: As we tune our transmitters and clear out circuits that do not serve us well by replacing them with new ones, we get moments of graced opportunity to experience the transcendent call of the Mind (pure mind). Our transmitters pick up "new frequencies" and experience things that go way beyond our everyday senses. As a result, we realize that life itself is more than our daily lives. We experience an innate call to discover our true identity, and to embrace our deepest potential. We also come to realize that we have courage, self-forgetfulness, and an ability and innate desire to contribute to and be part of the universal good. We have a new appreciation of relationship and time.

These realizations are some of the pure mind's attributes shining through. By continuously tuning our transmitters, we open pathways to the "pure mind," the infinite Mind, the Mind that is the heart of it all.

Chapter 5

Meditation: The Foundation of Mindfulness

THE ECSTASY AND AGONY OF MEDITATION

The Ecstasy

Many years ago, I was working with a client in Lyon, France. It was a treat to fly there every week to help them with a radical restructuring of their organization. One week, I decided that instead of flying, I would drive from my home in London, take the ferry from Dover to Calais, and continue onward by car down to Lyon. This was a long haul, but the beautiful French scenery and the efficient road system, made it worthwhile. And of course, it was easy to get beakers of French champagne along the way!

On this particular trip, I had decided to stay in France a few days longer. My goal was to visit the town of Taize, a small town not far from the historical village of Cluny renowned for its magnificent Abbey and monastery.

The story of Taize is an inspiring one. Amidst the terror, persecution and carnage of the Second World War, a few men got together to create an ecumenical monastic order dedicated to providing a sanctuary and hiding place for refugees. They created the town of Taize, a small cluster of outbuildings buried in the French countryside.

The town was founded on a brotherhood of love, acceptance and reverence for God. Very soon it became known as a home open to anyone in distress. Hundreds of people were saved through the care of the Taize community.

Fast forward fifty years to the nineteen nineties, and Taize had become famous as an ecumenical meditation town. Everyone was welcome, and people from all over the world came for the Taize experience.

The Friday I arrived, cars, vans, trucks, and buses were battling like me to find parking on the open fields that surrounded the Taize buildings. People of every nationality, race, color, creed, age, and description converged on a massive tent in the middle of this collection of simple buildings.

When I entered the tent, it reminded me of my encounter in Bangkok, except this was different. There were hundreds of people sitting, crouching, kneeling, praying, and meditating. No one spoke. In the background, I could hear the wonderful chant of the Taize monks. I was mesmerized. Here were all these hundreds of people, drawn from everywhere in the world, silently meditating together. For hours we sat in that tent, surrendering to the chant and to the energy of mutual connection through silence. It was a deeply moving experience of spiritual ecstasy.

Meditation can offer us these wonderful moments of peace, calm, relaxation and inner surrender. Through deep breathing, we gain poise and perspective. We get up from meditation feeling refreshed and enlivened—no matter how much our time of quiet sitting challenged us. Meditation can truly be an experience of bliss.

The Agony

However, there is another side to meditation. Sitting in silence, where the mind rests and studies itself, is not easy. We learn about ourselves in ways that are both shocking and transformative.

Meditation is one of our greatest teachers, especially in humility. As we sit in silence and get to experience our monkey-mind frantically jumping everywhere, we come to realize many things.

We realize we are fearful. We realize we are control freaks, we are fundamentalists, we are prejudiced, we are fixated on the small stuff, we are terrified of the big stuff, we are short-sighted, we are agitated, stressed, anxious, and we have ADHD (attention deficit hyperactivity disorder). We worry about yesterday. We worry about tomorrow. If we get a chance, we worry about today. We run as fast as we can from the present moment. We run, hide, rationalize, plan, organize... whew!

This is no ecstasy. It is sheer agony!

Many people say they just cannot meditate. It is too much. The noise in their heads is too frightening and too distracting. They feel it is better not to get in touch with what is really going on inside. Some even blame meditation for making them agitated, convincing themselves that they are not this stressed and frantic person. Learning how their mind really works is just too hard.

MEDITATION IS THE GREAT STRESS REDUCER

I urge those of you who find meditation too daunting to "hang in there." Every effort you make to meditate helps. Every moment you struggle pays off. Every time you bring your mind back to your breath, your mind is getting signals that something different is happening. It may be imperceptible at first, but slowly, slowly, every minute of meditation changes your brain and slows down your jumping mind. Every minute of meditation helps to reduce stress. It is a matter of trusting the process. And moments of ecstasy come when one least expects it.

I mentioned in previous chapters that mindfulness and meditation are great antidotes to stress and anxiety. Doctors report that over eighty percent of all illnesses are due in some way or another to stress. If we can reduce stress in our lives, it can make a huge impact on how we live and everything we do.

Meditation is a great stress reducer. It has been found to be more relaxing than almost any other method of relaxation. Its impact on the brain and the immune system has now been well-researched. Experiments show that even small amounts of time, such as 10-15 minutes a day, consistently dedicated to meditation, can result in significant health benefits.

Find the will power and the discipline to meditate. Begin with small steps. You will be so glad you did!

MEDITATION AS THE BASIS OF MINDFULNESS

Whether we like it or not, if we want to be mindful people, we need to engage in meditation. It is by meditating that we develop our abilities to stay aware and be attentive to the present moment. It is by meditating that we train the mind to calm down and pay attention with intention. It is by meditating that we gain enormous insights in self-awareness. It is by meditating that we increase our gray matter. It is by meditating that we rewire our brains.

Think of meditation as the gym or exercise routine for the mind. Meditation helps build the mindfulness muscles. The marvelous thing with meditation is that unlike the gym, one does not need different clothes or equipment, nor does one need to drive anywhere. We can meditate in any place, at any time, dressed in anything or nothing!

UNDERSTANDING MEDITATION

Many people fall into the trap of thinking that meditation is yet another thing they have to do. That is an unfortunate misunder-standing. On the contrary. Meditation is a non-doing. Nothing extra needs to be done. Rather, meditation is a being; a being just where you are, as you are, as you get to know your inner life, and how you create and construe your reality. Meditation is the best way to find your inner temple or sanctuary.

Another way to understand meditation is that it is an undoing, a yielding, a letting go. It is a time to drop everything and just be. This letting go releases us from all our tensions and constrictions, allowing us to integrate our mind, body, and breath.

There is also a tendency among many of us to think that meditation is a "mind job." This is another fallacy. We are integrally connected to our bodies. In fact, we are our bodies. As we discussed in the previous chapter, our bodies are as much our minds, as are our heads, where most of us tend to think our minds are located. Meditation calls for an integration of mind, body, and soul. Meditation assists the functioning and vitality of all three.

Meditation is also about relationship. We meditate to know ourselves. It is a process of coming into relationship with our own consciousness. Like any other intimate relationship, meditation requires commitment, time, patience and tolerance. If we cannot give this to ourselves, how can we imagine we can give this to others?

Finally, meditation is a practice. It is most effective if it becomes part of everyday life. It should not be viewed as an escape from reality, but as another way of encountering reality in a very personal and special way. The wonderful thing about this practice is that one can never fail. The only possible failure is not showing up.

Everything that happens during meditation is grist for the self-awareness mill. Nothing is lost and nothing is a waste of time. There is only one proviso, and that is that one tries with a non-judgmental, open heart. Each time you try counts. Each time you try, your brain is reminded of this new neural connection. Each time you try, you are showing self-mastery. Each time you try, imperceptibly at first, things begin to change. Each time you try, you are making a personal statement about the kind of person you want to be. Each time you try, you can say "I did it!"

MEDITATION IN A NUTSHELL
- It is a non-doing
- It is a letting go
- It is a mind-body engagement
- It is a development of a relationship with oneself
- It is a practice
- It is a major stress reducer

THE BREATH: A FRIEND FOR LIFE
As a young child, I hated being sick. Both my parents had to work

and, much as they wanted to, they could rarely stay at home and take care of me. So, I would be alone. Sometimes I would be frightened to be sick and alone. One day I discovered a friend that would be with me all the time, even when I was sick. That was my breath. When I would lie in bed feeling miserable and sorry for myself, I would pull the covers over my head and begin to breathe deeply. This activity gave me great peace and reassurance. I would talk to my breath. It became my best friend. I gave my breath a name. When I was feeling miserable, I would breathe in and out, saying the name over and over again. It would soothe and calm me and always bring down my temperature. Little did I know that I was actually meditating and that I had created my own mantra. Little did I know I was using my breath to heal myself.

Now, many, many years later, I have come to appreciate more than ever the value of one's breath. I have also learned that every wisdom or religious tradition considers the breath to be sacred. Our breath is our life. The first breath signals the beginning of life, and the last breath the end. We live between these two defining portals.

OUR BREATH HEALS

One Breath at a Time

Many years ago, I was the Finance professor at a graduate school in Boston that offered MBA programs aimed only at women. I count myself fortunate in that I have always loved mathematics, and have had a reasonable aptitude for the subject. From a young age, my parents encouraged me to develop this aptitude. Many of the women in my finance class were not so fortunate. They either had no feel for the subject, or had no interest. Some had sadly been told at a young age that "numbers" were for men, and that they should focus on more womanly pursuits such as human resources management, public relations, secretarial skills, and so on.

As part of their finance requirement, each student had to make several presentations to the class on some financial matter using the jargon of finance while explaining a financial calculation. In my first year of teaching the MBA finance class, I was simply horrified to learn how traumatic this experience was for many of the women students. I discovered, to my dismay, that before the class, the restrooms would be full of students being ill in one way or another.

There was one young woman that I was most concerned about. She was thin as a rail, and always looked terribly stressed. Of her own volition, one day she appeared in my office. She shared a most shocking story of her life, one part of which was that her father did not want her to be better in mathematics than her two brothers. The reality was that she was quite brilliant and could calculate anything. She grasped all the finance concepts in a flash, and was way ahead of the others in the class. However, she hid in the back row and never said a word. When it came to presenting to the class, the flashback of the beatings and humiliation by her father all but gagged her. She would spend the morning vomiting in the bathroom.

I listened carefully realizing that this situation was way beyond my skills and my contract with the student. I suggested she see the college counselor, which went nowhere. She said she had spent a fortune on counselors and that she was done with them and their medications.

I suggested meditation. She said she would try provided I stayed with her the first few times as she was afraid. So twice a week we sat in my office mediating and I taught her to breathe. I gave her a series of breathing exercises and we practiced her breathing before she would present to a class. I would tell her "concept by concept—one breath at a time." This became her mantra.

Four weeks later, I suggested she now do this alone and with a friend or fellow student. By the end of the year, she was a different person. She spoke up in class and made some eloquent and thoughtful presentations. She had stuck to her mantra: "concept by concept—one breath at a time."

THE POWER OF DEEP BREATHING

Neuroscience is now proving with science what the ancients have known for ages. The Chinese, with their *Qi Kung* and *Tai Chi* exercises, have been teaching breath training for centuries. All this comes down to one thing: Our breath has enormous healing power.

Deep breathing activates the parasympathetic nervous system (we met this in Chapter 4—it is the brake on our anxiety mechanism). It has a hugely calming effect. The longer we can breathe out, the better. Breathing out for as long as possible, is what really matters.

Deep, diaphragmatic breathing, where we hold our breath for a few counts as we breathe in, and then breathe out, slowly and for as long as we can, is very healthy for us. It reduces our heart rate, reduces blood pressure, strengthens and expands our lungs, improves our circulation which is the great healing agent, and calms our minds. People who have been in critically ill situations have healed themselves through the power of breathing. There is no end to what we are finding out about our breath. It truly is our best friend. And it is our lifelong and most loyal friend.

Mindfulness, and especially meditation, teaches us the transforming impact of working consciously with our breath. By mindfully breathing, we find a new understanding of who we are and how we engage in the world.

MEDITATING ON THE BREATH

Most meditation practices suggest that we focus on our breath as it makes its passage in and out of our bodies. The idea is to use the breath as an anchor for our thoughts. It gives our monkey-mind something to pay attention to. We are told to focus on the in-breath and to learn about it. Where does it go? What does it feel like as it travels through the body? Is it long, short, deep, shallow, fast, slow? Is one in-breath different from the next? If so, how? Then the out-breath. What does that feel like? Where does it move through our body? Is it long, short, deep, shallow, fast, slow? And so we pay attention to one breath after another.

There are several reasons we use our breath as our anchor of attention. For one, our breath is with us every moment of every day. We can access it at any time. It is also embodied. By focusing on it, we remain in our bodies and do not disappear into our heads. Our breathing occurs moment by moment. So, by paying attention to our breath, we are paying attention to each moment by moment. It forces us to be in the present.

By staying with the breath, moment by moment, we can also observe our minds jumping around between the past and the future. We get to see our fixations, attachments, fears, phobias, assumptions and expectations. In other words, we learn about how we have conditioned our minds.

During meditation, a most important thing we practice is to learn about ourselves without passing judgment. We do not add beating ourselves up to the rest of our mind-created dramas. We learn about ourselves non-judgmentally. That is not easy! However, if we stick to our meditation practice, we get better and better at it. The payoff is huge. We come to learn compassion for ourselves. And it is only when we have compassion for ourselves, that we can have genuine compassion and understanding for others. We explore this further in Chapter 8 where we discuss "Managing Organizations and Mindful Virtues."

BODY SCAN

To get ourselves settled for meditation, we can begin with a body scan. This is described in more detail in Appendix 1. Essentially the body scan brings our attention into the body and helps us find those places that are knotted, tight or constricted. By breathing into those spots, we can release tension, free energy and begin to attend to our breath.

We begin the scan by starting with the front of our body, our nostrils, and then become aware of how our breath moves progressively into the center of our body and our being. Breathing in we take the outer world in. We integrate it into ourselves and then let the breath leave us again. This exercise helps us become more aware of the mystery of the space within our bodies, and we become aware of the entire body as an organ of breathing.

CONSCIOUS BREATHING LEADS TO RELAXATION

By meditating on and with the breath, we can truly start to let go. As our breathing becomes calmer, the internal dialog of our minds begins to settle down. From this position of quiet alertness, it becomes possible to view one's own stream of consciousness. The awareness that in normal living is focused outward, is now turned inward. During this process we learn to separate our thoughts and feelings from our deepest selves. We become aware of the contents of our minds and realize they are not us. As we discussed in Chapter 2, we realize that we can choose what we want to identify with.

Over time, as we meditate, the compulsive habits of thought—many of them based on fear, desire, neediness, and self-centeredness—begin to lose their power. A new self-identity begins to form, one based on less reactive awareness.

This repeated attention to our own awareness begins to free us of our compulsions and inappropriate thoughts and behavior. As we focus on our breathing, we unlock the tight parts we are holding in our inner most self. Paying attention to the breath in this deep way helps us bring together our body, mind, and breath so that we become more whole and more alive to who we really are. That is the power of meditation. That is also the goal of mindfulness.

DEALING WITH THOSE DARN DISTRACTIONS

All this sounds well and good. But, as we discussed earlier, our minds are not as compliant as we would like them to be. The monkey-mind jumps all over the place taking us as far away from our breath and body as it can. The mind wants to plan, to make shopping lists, to think of the vacation, to get mad at John, and to remind us of yesterday's mess-ups.

Try as we might, after a second or two of focus, the mind is at it again. The more we sit, the more the mind seems to jump. We tell ourselves that we cannot stand it. We need to distract this monkey-mind. BUT the monkey-mind is the distraction!

The true natural mind is as clear as an unruffled pond. It is calm, it is open and spacious. It enjoys peace and silence. It is present.

What is hard to acknowledge is that the monkey-mind is how we are functioning most of the time. We are just not aware of it because we are not paying attention. That is why we need five emails to confirm one appointment, four pulls on the handle to check we have locked the door, meetings after meetings to pick up what we did not really pick up at the meeting, follow up notices and reminders for the many things we do… and we still do not get more than fifty percent of what we committed to correct the first time. Typical distractions include:

- Monkey-mind—the mind running amuck in many directions
- Difficulty with concentration
- Bodily discomfort—itching, twitching, inability to sit still
- Noise from the outside that cannot be shut out
- Inability to keep the spine straight
- Drowsiness or falling asleep
- Boredom
- Unwholesome thoughts
- Discouragement

STRATEGIES TO HELP FOCUS

Here are some strategies to help persevere with meditation without giving up.

- Use a mantra—say a precious word, over and over again, as you focus on the breath
- Count your breaths as they move through you, staying with the breath as you count it
- Engage in six to ten deep breaths, counting four as you breathe in, hold for four, and breathe out for the count of four

- Visualize something inside—this could be light, or warmth, or love
- Set an intention—dedicate your meditation to loving kindness or forgiveness or to healing some part of yourself or someone else
- Set your concentration on the breath as if you were cutting something with a very sharp knife
- Meditate on a specific distraction that comes up—for example fear, or anger, or grief
- Do whatever you can to not give up! Stay with your experience and keep asking yourself: What can I learn here? You will find there is always something to learn. We might not like what we learn about ourselves, yet that learning has huge transforming power. It gets us to know ourselves. It gives us both humility and courage—and therein lies our freedom and our humanity

MEDITATION: GETTING GOING

Here are a few basic ideas and guidelines. I prefer to stay away from strict rules as that brings up the idea of failing or non-compliance. Meditation is a very personal affair and needs to meld with the personality of the individual.

- Find a separate space somewhere at home or in your office where you can create a personal boundary
- Try to find a place with the least noise
- Pick a regular time each day that fits in with your personal rhythm and your daily obligations
- If you sit on a cushion on the floor, be sure your hips are higher than your knees. This helps lessen the strain on your back
- If you use a chair, be sure it has a straight back
- Sit upright, spine erect but not uptight
- Keep your head in a position as if a thread is holding it up from the ceiling. It should be aligned with your back

- If you are sitting in a lotus position, find one that does not stress your back or knees. If you are sitting on a chair, be sure to have a straight spine with feet flat on the floor — preferably without shoes
- Place your hands on your thighs or hold them gently folded in your lap
- Breathe normally
- Your eyes can be open or closed. If you keep them open, fixate on some place six to eight feet in front of you. Hold the eyes gently
- Use a timer so that you are not worrying about time
- Try not to move, scratch, itch or shift around during your allotted sitting time. Find patience and curiosity about your discomfort. Do not push into any serious pain. Rearrange yourself if a pain persists
- Try to meditate in pure silence. From time to time you can use music or a guided meditation. It is preferable not to rely on these distractions for every session. The mind and the soul truly revel in silence
- Anchor your attention on your breath. Be aware of it — we describe how below — and watch it, listen to it, get to know it. Your breath is your most intimate and enduring partner

THE IMPORTANT MATTER OF POSTURE

Our Body Reflects Our Minds

With meditation, we learn a lot about how our bodies and minds work together. An uptight body produces an uptight mind! A sloppy body reflects a sloppy mind! The posture we adopt when we meditate, both activates and reacts to our attitude or disposition. If we are feeling happy, our body is upright, open and perky. If we are feeling grouchy, our neck is pulled in, our shoulders are tight, and our face is grim. Our bodies and minds are integrated.

An alert, vibrant, and adaptive mind is reflected in a body that is composed, flexible, and resilient. The reverse is also true. What we want to do when we meditate is get our bodies in the most alert, open, and calm position possible.

Alignment is Key

A very important part of meditation is bodily alignment. I have found that many people struggle to sit up straight, with their feet flat on the floor, and stay in that position for several minutes. It does not take long before the back sags, the feet begin twitching, the ankles get crossed, and the head falls forwards or backwards. Many people end up fighting off sleep.

I encourage people to try to stay in an erect—but not uptight—position for as long as possible. I suggest imagining a thread passing from the ceiling through the center of one's head, going down through one's body, down to the center of the earth in a straight line.

Why is this uprightness so important? There are a few reasons: Our spinal cord is a vital link between the body and the brain. By keeping our spine upright, we expand our lung capacities and our undistorted or curved spine allows for a steady, easy flow of signals between body and brain.

Our spine also carries or transmits what is referred to as our kundalini energy. If our kundalini energy can move from the base of our sacrum freely through an upright spine, we can harness the different types of body and psychic energy in many powerful ways. We are also more likely to experience spiritual insights.

An upright spine also helps us align our bodies with the gravitational center of the earth. The more aligned we are, the less our muscles need to work to keep us sitting up straight. The body uses the earth's energy for this alignment rather than its own.

Lastly, an upright spine, with the head held horizontally, enables greater alertness. Once we let our heads sag, it is so much easier to become drowsy or distracted.

Relaxation

It seems counter-intuitive, but the more relaxed we are, the more aware we can be.

Relaxation means not having tension in our bodies. Tension has a direct impact on our breathing. The more tightly we hold ourselves, the more restricted our breathing. Tension also distracts our mind. A tight body results in a tight mind. A relaxed body enables the mind to be in communication and acknowledge the sensations pulsating throughout the body. Tight sensations are inhibiting. Relaxed sensations are warming, encouraging, and freeing. The more our life force can flow through our bodies, the more easily we can breathe and the more spacious and free our minds will be. Relaxation denotes a safe surrender. A safe surrender, allows consciousness to emerge behind the frantic antics of the monkey-mind. Just relax!

Try this out:

Try sitting or walking with an erect and aligned posture. Breathe into your body normally. Relax your shoulders, open your chest, gentle your face muscles, and feel the subtle movement of your body. How does your mind feel? What thoughts come up?

Sit slouched, with one elbow on the desk. Screw up your face, hunch your shoulders, cross your ankles, and sit tight. How does your mind feel now? What thoughts come up?

MEDITATION: CREATING A PRACTICE

Here are a few ideas that may help get you begin or continue a sustaining practice.

- Create a ritual around your practice. Read a poem, light a candle or incense, chant a song, pray for someone you love. You can do this before or afterwards or both
- Treat each period as an interesting opportunity to get to know yourself and to strengthen your relationship with yourself
- Consider the time you set aside as an adventure or an unusual journey—what will come up?

- Use the time to see how you can experience deep relaxation by watching your breath. Savor the relaxation
- Dedicate the time to a specific intentional meditation. For example, focusing on love, or light, or forgiveness
- Treat your time as a learning experience. Keep a journal, and after meditating, record what the experience was like, and ask yourself what you have learned about yourself
- When you find your mind is driving you mad, find humor. "There you go again Annabel. And you thought you were the cat's meow!"
- At the end of your meditation time, try not to rush into the next thing, but honor the time you spent with yourself. You might even say something to yourself like, "Tom—you have come a long way."

Chapter 6
Mindful Leadership

IN THE TANK

A few years ago, the CEO of a technical design company, ABC Inc. (not its real name), engaged me to help the Board of the company—made up of working partners—deal with what he called "significant new realities." As is usually the case, what we often define as new realities are old ones. We were just not paying attention.

My assignment was a leadership and change challenge. The Board members of ABC were refusing to accept and respond to a rapidly diminishing work pipeline, not to mention a hugely changing work environment. They were convinced that some enormous new project was going to arrive imminently from somewhere. It always had in the past, so why the fuss?

ABC employed over a hundred highly specialized engineers who worked on all kinds of projects related to the oil industry. They designed project sites, tanker loading and offloading docks, as well as sections of oil rigs.

The market was a complex one. Projects were usually part of a package that included other partners and subcontractors. This made pricing and meeting deadlines challenging. Due to the complexity, size, and regulations associated with all designs, securing a project involved a long lead time. From proposal to the final award of a project could take up to twenty months. Once the project was secured, however, the work and the money poured in for several years.

Three years prior to recruiting my assistance, the market had changed significantly. Several of ABC's very large projects had ended. New overseas competitors had entered the market and challenged ABC's special niche. The Deep Water Horizon oil spill continued to dampen the enthusiasm for new oil sites and new tankers, so the number of projects out for bid had diminished. Oil prices had also fallen radically. And the day I sat down with the CEO of ABC, his forecasts showed that the organization's revenue had been dropping for the past eighteen months and would plunge by sixty percent within the next year! Cash flow projections allowed for eight months of operations at lower revenue levels. And he called this "new realities!"

I attended the next Board meeting to learn about the Board's resistance and to devise possible ways to get the organization to react with radical urgency. Some Board members were openly antagonistic and clearly disliked the fact that I had been hired. After a very direct presentation on my part, which included several rapid downsizing scenarios with actionable steps, I managed to convince half the Board in favor of doing something. Even so—it was too late in the game. Added to that, when it came to follow through, the partners sabotaged one another, fought for their departments, clung to their high salaries, and generally continued to deny what was right in front of them.

Sadly, as I predicted—who would not have?—the firm had to lay off half its staff within three months. The CEO had a heart attack. The COO had a nervous breakdown. Some staff, claiming stress, sought to take medical leave, to no avail. The CFO jumped ship. And this forty-year-old, once thriving, niche organization, known for excellent work and good values, closed its doors. A few remaining engineers were absorbed into other companies. A sad tale indeed.

Although this is a highly abbreviated version of the whole saga, what we can learn from this and our discussion in Chapter 1 is as follows:

- New realities are always arriving
- New realities are often ruthless

- Detecting new realities as early as possible is critical to the survival of any organization
- Denying new realities has a high price
- A primary task of leadership is paying attention

THE NEW REALITIES

Everything has changed except our way of thinking.
- Albert Einstein

As we discussed in Chapter 1, we live in a topsy-turvy world. Everything is in flux. It seems as if we are swimming in a churning sea with no shore in sight. Leaders are confronted with new problems that demand new solutions. What worked before does not work now. We need to change our thinking.

New realities, and especially paradigm shifts, demand adaptive rather than technical solutions. Adaptive solutions refer to personal transformation. Technical solutions refer to procedures, routines and skills. Before I expand on the distinction between adaptive and technical work, let us review some of the specific new realities clamoring for attention.

Work is not Working

Many organizations are experiencing troubling times at work. There are, for example, employee engagement problems, performance problems, resource allocation problems, ethical problems, stress-related problems, and as always, communication problems. Many employees complain of long hours at work with little real added value to show for it. Anxiety and stress punctuate our times. And, despite our commitment as a nation to the pursuit of happiness, we are not very happy!

Based on the statistics, the present generation of young people are more emotionally troubled than the last. They are more lonely, depressed, nervous, worried, impulsive, and aggressive than the generations before them. And then of course we have the drug-related problems.

In the United States, the incidence of suicide among fifteen to twenty-four-year-olds tripled in the last half of the twentieth century. In 2016, suicide rates reached the highest point in nearly thirty years in the general population. For middle aged adults, suicide has increased forty percent since 1999. Each year, 40,000 Americans take their lives, and worldwide nearly one million people commit suicide.

A reading of the contemporary business literature such as Forbes Magazine, Fortune, and The Harvard Business Review, reveals that finding meaning and purpose is a central issue for many employees and their bosses. People are increasingly looking to work to fulfill their emotional and psychological lives. It seems the millennials are particularly demanding about finding meaning at work. The need for daily bread has taken on new symbol and form. The family, Church, or Temple that used to provide the containing function is no longer useful to many. The official workplace has become for many the place for meaning and succor.

As an executive coach, I am exposed to many people's lives at work. Many express confusion and being overwhelmed as they struggle to meet the increasing demands made by their organizations. They also talk about greater stresses in their home lives.

I find that a high percentage of people do not seem to question how they make meaning every day. Daily life is one mad rush determined by the alarm clock, daily duties, and email imprisonment. Many do not have what I call a philosophy of life, nor do they have a physical, psychological, or emotional sanctuary where they can find nourishment and rest for the soul. Trouble at home tumbles over into trouble at work, and vice versa. There seems to be no escape from the "bedlam of the Bangkok streets."

In response to these challenges, many organizations are introducing new employee engagement programs in efforts to make the workplace more relaxed and appealing. Companies are investing in new aesthetic layouts, lounges, in-house coffee shops, and even bars to make the work place "homey" and attractive. In addition, managers are being charged with developing visionary slogans and statements of purpose that will supposedly make work meaningful.

Alas, these are technical fixes for adaptive problems. Let us explore what this means.

ADAPTIVE PROBLEMS NEED ADAPTIVE SOLUTIONS

Adaptive problems arise from new realities that challenge our existing way of being, living or working. Well, you could say that all problems fall into one of those categories. That is correct. All problems, in some way — either at a minuscule level or more substantially — have an adaptive component.

What makes something an adaptive problem is that to respond to it adequately requires a different consciousness, a new way of thinking. One could say it is a new way of understanding oneself and the world. Let us take ABC Inc. as an example. Their adaptive challenge was that, in order to survive in their changing world, they needed to recalibrate and reinvent who they were as an organization. They needed to see themselves and their role in their industry differently. They would have to learn a new way of being, of self-understanding and thus of operating. They needed to learn new competencies. Their identity needed to change, as did their business model.

In essence, adaptive problems have these components:

- They challenge our existing understanding of ourselves and our identity
- They require a new way of being, of self-understanding, and of consciousness
- They force us to relinquish existing habitual patterns of thought and behavior
- They place the relevance of our role and our current competency under question. Invariably, new competencies are required

- They require us to learn something in order to address the challenge
- They require transformation not just change

Examples of adaptive problems include: climate change, the refugee crisis, disruption of industries, AI and advanced robotics, healthcare, moving to 24/7 operations, loss of meaning, stress, chronic illness, low engagement, unhappiness, and ADHD.

Paradigm shifts in any dimension or domain always demand adaptive solutions prior to technical ones.

By contrast, technical problems focus on doing. They relate to technical and procedural work. Examples include: the need for updated software, new maintenance programs, a revised strategic plan, a new organizational chart, new procedures and protocols, or buying a new car.

As you can see, adaptive problems are different from technical ones. It is not a matter of which is better or worse. We encounter both adaptive and technical problems and we need both adaptive and technical solutions. Adaptive solutions invariably need the support of some technical work. They go together. But the one cannot supplant the other. Failing to identify *which* solution is needed *when* results in big problems down the line. Believe me!

If one is not paying attention, the new realities that swiftly become old realities force us into reactive mode, so we never address the real problem! We simply rush from one technical fix to the next. ABC Inc. is one sad example.

THE TASKS OF THE MINDFUL LEADER

Paying Attention

Leadership is primarily concerned with identifying new realities, preferably when they are new. The rest of the leadership work such as vision, strategy, planning, decision-making, empowering others, having emotional intelligence and so on, all flow from the leader/s aligning the organization with the changing environment. Without that primary focus, there will—like ABC, Inc.—be no organization!

Leadership is thus about paying attention. Not any old attention. But exquisite attention. Attention to what is arising each moment within the spheres of the relevant domains at the time.

This attention is a mindful attention. It is an open, unbiased, questioning and curious attention. If it does not have this quality, then whatever new is arising will not be clearly identified. It will be a conditioned projection of past experiences. And the same worn out solutions will be applied.

Leading Change

The role of leadership is largely concerned with the facilitation of change. Change begins with the arrival of new realities. Change is challenging mostly because of the adaptive work it entails. Technical work is much easier than adaptive work. It is much easier to do new things than to be different.

Mindful leadership is about differentiating the adaptive work from the technical work and aligning people appropriately around the tasks involved. The change process, as we have all experienced, is often uncomfortable. Leadership here must demonstrate commitment, grit, understanding of the gains and losses, empathy, and an ability to maintain focus amidst the tensions and distractions that are frequently created. As we discussed in earlier chapters, mindfulness and meditation build these strengths.

Being a Learner

Effective leaders are learners. They are not only readers of books, but readers of situations. They pay attention and learn. They learn from the environment. They learn from employees. They learn from their customers, their suppliers, and their competitors. They learn from the present moment, from whatever is taking place right before them. They are paying mindful attention.

Articulating a Vision

Leaders read the new realities and can, with the help of others, articulate a vision of future possibilities. They have imagination. They are not constrained by the past. They are not intimidated by the future. They guide today's work into the shaping of tomorrow's world. They live into the future by paying exquisite attention to what is happening now. They are centered, focused, and mindful. (We talk about vision some more in Chapter 10.)

Role Modeling

Leaders are most effective when they lead by example, when they walk their talk.

Tom Raffio of Delta Dental is renowned for this, and that is what makes his leadership so effective. He does not say very much. In fact, he is one of the least talkative leaders I know. Yet, he gets a mountain achieved. How? Simply through role modeling.

There is the old saying, you can only fool some of the people some of the time. True role modeling is sincere. It is not a posing or posturing. People know when it comes from a core center, an authenticity, an inner ground. There is a certain poise and equanimity that come with it. Mindfulness, as we discussed in Chapters 1 and 2, helps one find and hold onto that center.

LEADERSHIP IS AN INSIDE-OUT JOB

Leading Oneself

To lead others begins with one's ability to lead oneself. That, as we know, begins with self-awareness. The self-awareness I am talking about is not a superficial one, but a deep one. This is a self-awareness where one has faced our inner monsters and has come to appreciate our inner gods. This is a self-awareness that develops humility and the strength to be vulnerable. This is a self-awareness that understands that life is a journey of inner discovery and that the inner journey mirrors the outer.

Mindfulness, and particularly meditation, develops and deepens that journey. In fact, there is nothing to beat meditation when it comes to self-awareness. As Bessel Van der Kolk, whom we met in Chapter 4 says, all growth and healing begin with self-awareness. Self-awareness in and of itself is a great health and healing agent. There is also nothing like it to ground our sense of self and to give us a perspective and courage to deal with life's challenges.

An Affair of the Heart

Effective leaders are positive and optimistic without being excessively enthusiastic. They are gracious. They appreciate themselves and know how to appreciate others. They are in love with life and with people. There is an innate desire to serve, to be open, to encourage and to develop others.

Having this disposition genuinely and consistently requires good self-care and good health. Stress, anxiety, and poor health ruin one's abilities to be in love. Mindful leaders know this and take the time to rest in their inner sanctuaries or shrines away from the bedlam of the streets.

NORTHEAST DELTA DENTAL'S PATH TO MINDFULNESS

Over the past year, Delta Dental has engaged in a variety of activities as part of its mindfulness initiative. Its approach has been to encourage a mindful disposition and the practice of mindfulness by making it part of the fabric of daily existence.

Delta Dental offered a Mindful Leadership program as part of its overall leadership and development training. Reinforcement of mindfulness is achieved through mindfulness and meditation sessions offered to the entire team—even those at a distance via teleconference—for a period of ninety minutes at a time. This is part of ongoing training and development.

A special mindfulness program was developed for managers where the focus was on how they could reduce stress, distraction, multitasking and errors in their departments. The internal newsletter now includes a Mindfulness Corner. Tom, frequently sends emails to all employees that includes some comment or reminder about the benefits of mindfulness.

Every week, I send a mindfulness blog to the Delta Dental participants. Tom has hosted some mindfulness feedback/focus group sessions with some of the employees. Recently, Delta Dental hosted a day of Delta Dental talks. The focus of the day was on mindful speaking, mindful listening, and having difficult conversations mindfully.

This subtle but permeating approach has had a most beneficial effect on many people and on many departments.

DELTA DENTAL'S MINDFULNESS PRACTICE

Employees of Delta Dental are encouraged to embrace some, preferably all, of these mindfulness practices each day. You can read in what follows how they find these helpful.

- To find opportunities, especially first thing in the morning or last thing at night, to experience silence For example, driving without the radio or music
- To practice mindful breathing first thing in the morning and throughout the day
- To practice mindful transitioning between activities and appointments
- To stretch periodically though out the day
- To set the intention to pay attention mindfully
- To make email appointment times at certain times during the day
- To practice mindful emailing—as discussed in Chapter 9
- To be a non-judgmental witness to one's feelings and thoughts whenever one can
- To listen and speak mindfully
- To practice openness and curiosity
- To end each day with a few moments of gratitude and an open heart

THE RETURN ON INVESTMENT

I have been gratified by stories from the participants of the mindfulness sessions at Delta Dental. Here are some of the stories:

"I had never heard of mindfulness before. But in three months, I have slowed down. I am less stressed and less judgmental. I am now discussing this with my son, who has begun to remind me not to bring my cell phone to the dinner table. He and I have whole new conversations now."

"I am going through some personal challenges right now that really stress me out and make it difficult for me to focus at work. The mindfulness discussions and the bit of meditation is helping me manage my emotions. I find I can set my priorities better and to focus at work."

"Having these mindfulness classes at work is a most amazing gift. I find that I now stop from time to time and really listen and try to be mindful. It is an amazing wake-up call."

"Practicing mindfulness is not easy. I have begun talking about it at home and now my husband and I talk about it and try to practice it. We catch one another not being mindful and this has helped reduce so much stress. I feel better coming to work each morning."

"Mindfulness has helped me be more connected with people. I also find I am more in tune with my actions and catch myself more often when I am being thoughtless or less present. It has also helped me with my relationships at home where I would take out my stress. My new approach at work is to make a list of priorities and not to be distracted and try to multitask."

"Delta Dental takes such good care of their employees, and these mindfulness sessions are another way they are showing this. Since attending the sessions, I find I pay attention more often and I try to be mindful more intentionally. It makes the day at work so much richer."

"The other day I was faced with a very difficult situation. It pushed all my buttons and I could feel myself freezing and going numb inside. I suddenly remembered Annabel's discussions about breathing, and I began some deep long breaths. I also focused on a little mindfulness medallion she gave each one of us. And my anxiety dropped. I kept breathing. Suddenly I found that I was ok, and I could handle this problem just fine. I felt wonderfully empowered and a new confidence in myself."

At the end of each mindfulness session at Delta Dental, I had attendees fill out a questionnaire about the main things they learned. I was happy to see that they valued meditation as the most important skill or tool, because meditation is the foundation of mindfulness. Meditation received double the mentions of the other benefits. The attendees also valued several other skills: being in the moment without judgment, learning to unitask instead of multitasking, and listening more while being slower to speak.

Themes and Representative Quotes from the Questionnaire:

In answer to the question "What did you learn? Three key lessons stood out:

- Meditate—received double the vote of the other benefits
- Use Tai Chi movement and/or breathing to calm myself and clear my head
- Relax and take time to breathe each day
- Breathing techniques can calm and center me
- Meditation deals with stress and helps me let go
- Take time to meditate and relax
- Tai Chi is meditation in movement—a big win for those of us struggling to quiet our mind chatter
- Incorporate meditation into my daily schedule
- Relax and breathe when I am stressed
- Be in the moment without judgment
- Do not judge and let negative thoughts in
- Push away nagging moments
- Don't be so serious: let my thoughts go
- Be conscious that I should act with spontaneity and freedom
- Act in a non-judgmental fashion
- Slow down and think before acting
- Unitask, not multitask

- Do not do too many things at once
- Reduce multitasking. Adopt unitasking
- Unitasking equates to actually accomplishing more—not less
- I can accomplish more now with less effort
- Arrive and be present without distractions
- Listen and speak more mindfully

We shall discuss some of these aspects of mindfulness in detail in the chapters that follow.

What we can note, however, is that mindfulness practice changes lives. What greater ROI is there than that?

Chapter 7

Mindfulness— A Change Initiative

THE POWER OF CULTURE

> *Culture eats strategy for lunch*
> *- Peter Drucker*

Culture Rules

When it comes to developing a new strategy or initiating change, many CEOs and leaders underestimate and even neglect the influence of culture. Peter Drucker, the famous management guru, did not mince his words about culture's power. Culture, he said, is the primary source of resistance to change. Culture can and will destroy whatever appears to challenge its survival or the status quo—no matter how bad that might be.

Without the support of the organization's culture, all efforts at change are frankly going nowhere. As a leadership and change consultant, I wholeheartedly support Drucker's assertions. I have witnessed far too many occasions where culture simply devours rejected or disdained new initiatives or strategies.

Obviously, the more challenging the change initiative, the bigger the resistance. Top level buy-in and messaging plays a huge role in managing and defusing that resistance.

Introducing Mindfulness

Is introducing mindfulness a challenging initiative? I think many organizations would say "yes." Why? Because as we discussed, mindfulness challenges us to BE different. In general, we prefer to lose ourselves in the technicality of doing. We prefer "mindless" tasks that are not personally challenging and that do not ask us to reevaluate the kind of person we are. It's much easier to select things that come easily, that are routine, that we can master quickly, that do not require personal self-discipline or regulation. This tends to be human nature.

HOWEVER, all is not lost! As with my expert systems that I described in the introductory chapter, once many of us break the barrier of personal fear and resistance and get a taste of mindfulness, we are drawn in. We then need the support, encouragement, and opportunities to develop our mindfulness skills.

The big secret to success—no surprise again—is how the mindfulness initiative is introduced and whether some senior people in the organization will take it on and become role models. As always, leadership is all important.

IMPLEMENTATION CONSIDERATIONS

Here are some things to consider:
- Mindfulness as a process is subtle and intangible
- It relates to being and not doing
- In the short-term, it is difficult to measure
- It maybe threatening to highly sensate or high activity people who are only comfortable or can only act on data
- It can be dismissed as a fad
- Some people use stress and overwhelm as their anchor. They say this is how I am. They do not want to relinquish this crutch
- The effort can be sidetracked by getting all kinds of gadgets advocated by consumerism. With mindfulness, no gadgets are necessary

- Some people might misconstrue mindfulness as a chance to be less alert and less attentive
- There is no expertise to boast of—no-one gets first prize or a bonus
- There is no authority in mindfulness—no-one can tell others what to do
- The reward lies in the process itself—a deeper, more authentic engagement

It might be difficult initially to prove specifically that mindfulness boosts the bottom line. However, its implementation is far less expensive than most new initiatives. In a short period of time, the ROI can be enormous as many of our stories have indicated.

MINDFULNESS AS A CULTURAL CHANGE INITIATIVE

Because culture is so important, I have summarized some of the key facets of culture below. If one is planning a significant change initiative, it is a good idea to "check the boxes" to see that a significant number of the components of culture have been addressed.

Culture as the Glue of the Organization

Culture is the embodied values, principles and practices underlying the social fabric of an organization. Culture underpins the organization's actions and reactions, and connects stakeholders to each other and to the company's purpose and processes. Culture is the glue that holds an organization together and unites people around shared assumptions, beliefs, and practices.

Who shapes the culture of the organization? Everyone, yet none more so than the CEO and his or her senior leadership team. If the CEO is also the founder of the organization, his or her values will play an even more significant role.

COMPONENTS OF CULTURE

The Physical Aspect of Culture
This includes the phenomena one sees, hears, and feels. For example, the architecture of the buildings, the layout of the offices, the technology in use, the décor or aesthetic impact, the clothing and attire of employees, observable behaviors such as eating at desks or walking around without shoes.

Values
This includes attention to learning, people development, and expectations around participation and involvement. Here we also include customs and rituals, myths, legends, and stories depicting heroes or villains. Then there are the espoused ethics and values along with performance standards and etiquette.

Shared Assumptions
These include both the written and unwritten rules of the game, of which the latter typically predominate. There are group norms around engagement, acceptance, language and shared meanings. There are also rules as to what makes a person a group insider or outsider.

Levels of competency are usually spelled out in job descriptions; however, actual competency is often measured by unwritten yet commonly agreed upon criteria.

Employees tend to have mental models of the organization and how it does and should do its work. There are both clear, overt rules for rewards and punishment, and equally clear, yet covert rules. Everyone soon gets to know what really gets rewarded or punished and by whom. The same goes for power and status. What is shown on the organization chart frequently has little to do with where the real power lies.

Among shared assumptions are the culture's typical way of responding to changes in the environment. Then there are assumptions about what time means and how it can or cannot be used. People have ideas about what is reality and what is the official story line, which is some version of the truth. They know whom they believe and whom they don't and how public to be about their opinions.

There are also overt and covert assumptions about what is a promotable activity and what will get one fired. There are unwritten codes or assumptions about who can be recruited and who can be laid off. Some people will never be recruited and some never laid off, whatever the cause. Play and humor is also a key cultural determinant.

HOW NOT TO DO IT!

"We are offering a Mindfulness and Meditation program open to all employees for the next three months beginning on Wednesday, February 3. It will take place in our training room on the second floor, between 1:00 pm and 2:00 pm, every second Wednesday. What the heck! Give it a try. You have nothing to lose. Signed, CEO of Mindless Company"

The above is a memo sent by a CEO to 500 staff members. I duly showed up on the Wednesday and was met by a group of forty people — mostly women. We had our first engagement, and I handed out the curriculum for the following weeks.

The following session, the CEO showed up late and left early. He sat at the back of the room, mostly with his eyes closed. As the weeks progressed, unsurprisingly, the group dwindled down to a core ten who continued to come faithfully to every session.

I had of course suggested that we needed to support the initiative with more than just sessions every two weeks. The CEO was averse to "pushing this down people's throats as they have so much to do," and would not support newsletters or any other form of "promotion" as he called it. Despite pleas from the ten people, after the three months, the CEO felt that the program had not proved its ROI, and should be discontinued. I continue to receive emails from the disappointed employees to this day. One of them took the initiative and is hosting a small group on her own. Bravo!

NOT ANOTHER MANAGEMENT FAD

Employees need to understand that a mindfulness initiative is not another management fad. This is not a flavor of the week, but a genuine attempt at changing the culture at work for the better, from the inside out. The result will be healthier people, who think better, relate better, and perform better because they are more integrated, more embodied, and more present to everything they do.

It helps if organizational leadership connects the mindfulness initiative with any new realities the organization is facing. They might link mindfulness to the organization's creativity, competitiveness, vibrancy, and health. Or, they could connect it with better execution, enhanced customer engagement, or higher performance.

Leadership Commitment

Leadership can be very helpful here in some of the following ways:
- Demonstrating commitment by the CEO and his or her senior team
- Providing regular training and education
- Role modeling by encouraging mindfulness in meetings, emails, customer engagement, and any other form of communications
- Enlisting the support of the Board
- Linking mindfulness to organizational values, engagement, rewards, and promotable activities

Mindfulness is a new way of being, not just for the individual, but also for the organization. The two are mutually accountable to one another. Without that understanding, commitment will be inconsistent and achieving long term sustainability and true change will prove difficult.

IMPLEMENTATION STRATEGIES

How does one begin to nurture a culture of mindfulness? As I have mentioned repeatedly, it begins at the top. The CEO and his or her senior management team need to genuinely commit and take an interest in infusing the culture with a new form of awareness and attention. Introducing some training programs is often a constructive and helpful move; however, leadership must also participate. If this initiative is perceived as yet another tactic to get more efficiency out of the rank-and-file, it will not penetrate in any deep way.

Changing some of the organization's physical environment can make a real impact. Instead of stark white walls, some walls could be painted in gentle hues of peach or coral or light blue — soothing colors. Plants could be strategically placed. Perhaps there could be a waterfall or a fish tank in the atrium or lounge. The cafeteria could be made to look less functional with signs saying: "no cell phones" and photos of people eating mindfully.

Pictures of streams or forests, both known to have a positive physiological impact on people, might be hung in strategic places. Meeting rooms should be airy, open, light-filled spaces, where people can see the sky and nature close by. Perhaps there could be a room set aside where people can meditate or take a mindful break. There could be gentle music or chimes that ring from time to time.

Besides inviting consultants to help with the décor, there is nothing like asking the employees what kind of atmosphere would help them to slow down, relax, be less frenetic and anxious, yet calmly alert. Employee involvement is important.

Besides training programs and changes to the environment, there are many behavioral aspects that need to be addressed. These are discussed in the following chapters under listening, speaking, engagement, emailing, attending meetings and so on.

What is important to bear in mind is that mindfulness is a more attentive way of being. It is about being present in a certain way. Both the individual and the organization must develop that together. There is no standard blue print describing an expected outcome. The ultimate measure will be a deeper authenticity, a less stressed and frenetic workplace, heightened effectiveness, and a focused eye on the prize — healthy sustainability for all.

GETTING GOING

- Get leadership commitment and top leaders must participate
- Get buy-in from key employees and opinion leaders
- Identify new realities that could benefit from mindfulness
- Create a communication plan—newsletters, email reminders, posters, décor, etc.
- Consider training or mindfulness sessions open to all
- Identify key starting points—e.g. meetings, emailing, eating at work
- Consider how to involve everyone in the workforce
- Find ways to build in humor and play
- Keep reminding everyone that "we are all in this together"
- Highlight the physiological benefits when appropriate—e.g. stress reduction
- Find ways to measure progress. Invite employee involvement and encourage self-regulation and self-measurement. Measures of mindfulness success must be used
- Hold a town meeting every three or four months for the community to reflect on what has been learned

Chapter 8

Managing Organizations and Mindful Virtues

MANAGING AIN'T EASY

Managers, by dint of their role, frequently find themselves in the vortex of many colliding workplace tensions. They have to manage up, manage down, and manage across, while also keeping their eye on the bottom line. They have to deal with employee stress, the crisis of engagement, and the continuous struggle to do more with less. They are charged with creating an adaptive and creative culture where employees are expected to readily embrace change. And, they are on the continuous hunt for new, talented, disciplined, and reliable people.

Managers also assume multiple roles, many of which are in conflict. They have to exercise leadership and initiate change while also asserting formal authority to ensure order and stability. They are supervisors, mentors, and coaches, all roles which imply different relationships with their employees. They need to ensure their staff members are motivated and productive and that their supervisor's goals are met. They usually work long days and are expected to be available at all hours. Their job is one massive juggling act from morning to night.

Some specific challenges include:

- Dealing with continuous change

- Struggling to prioritize as everything seems urgent
- Feeling overwhelmed, which can inhibit effectiveness
- Maintaining employee engagement
- Sustaining productivity
- Ensuring inter-departmental teamwork
- Overcoming communication ineffectiveness
- Creating a climate that fosters resilience and creativity

This list (which is far from the full catastrophe!), is enough to make anyone apprehensive. I am sure that by now you can see that mindfulness can play a helpful and constructive role here.

MANAGING MEANS MANAGING PEOPLE

Managing means managing people. We manage people and we allocate resources. People are the heart and soul of any company. People provide the energy, the ideas, the intelligence, the commitment, the engagement and the soul of all institutions.

Mindful managers realize that the full person comes to work. However consciously people may be present, their full lives arrive at the doorstep or in front of the computer each day. Those full lives, just as one's own, carry a lot of energy, promise and hope as well as stress, confusion, or pain. The mindful manager knows this. That is why the mindful manager emphasizes importance in the development of self-awareness, emotional intelligence, and resilience for reasons we shall discuss.

The mindful manager is aware that people need some combination of certainty and variety. They need to feel a sense of significance and connection. They need opportunities for personal growth and a sense that they are making a worthwhile contribution. They also need some allowance for their humanity. We like to say that people are not machines, yet we treat them as such, especially when times are tough, and the bottom line is being squeezed.

In this chapter, I discuss some of the challenges managers face and I talk about what I call the mindfulness virtues. These virtues or qualities improve our functioning in life and at work. These qualities reinforce our inner strengths and make us more adaptive and more resilient. An adaptive and resilient workforce means an adaptive and resilient company.

MINDFULNESS IS SELF-AWARENESS

You can go within, or just go without.
- Viktor Frankl

Mindfulness is self-awareness. It is the continuous paying attention to who I am in every situation. It is not just about knowing our likes or dislikes, our Meyers-Briggs Type Indicator, or whether we are introvert or extrovert. These are of course important and interesting things to know and can be helpful when we are given certain tasks or assigned to teams. Real self-awareness is much more than that. It arises as a result of our witnessing and observing our feelings, thoughts and reactions.

Developing self-awareness is an inner exploration. This exploration uncovers things such as the number of conflicting "Is" that drive us hither and thither demanding at one moment this, and the next moment that. With this exploration, we also learn about our fears, insecurities, angers, desires, and motivations. We get in touch with our longing for unconditional love and acceptance and our need to be in connection and relationship.

Our inner exploration uncovers our ambivalences, our regrets, our unfinished business, and the shadow issues we project onto others. Our inner exploration exposes the many ways in which we self-sabotage by acting out our unworked through issues. This exploration also enables us to see our unquestioned assumptions, biases, and expectations.

Deep exploration also helps us see our hopes, dreams, and passions. It gives us a glimpse into the window of our souls that are longing for expression. It helps us see how much courage, self-forgetfulness, and humanity we possess when we are truly in touch with our deepest self. It helps us find our authenticity and it gives us an inner compass to keep striving for our own true north.

Delta Dental Employee Experiences of Self-Awareness

One claims analyst explained her reactions to the mindfulness sessions as follows:

"I believe that you can only be there for others if you are there for yourself first. It's the difference between being self-aware versus selfish. By listening without assumption, personally communicating, and building relationships it gives each of us an opportunity to be interested in others, which by default, I believe makes us more interesting. We must take care of ourselves first. If we take care of ourselves, we are more centered, calm and focused and can do more for others."

A technology analyst shared her views:

"People should attend the mindfulness seminar without an agenda. It will do more than you can expect. For instance, if you take the seminar to address a problem (such as road rage or how to be more productive on a project), you will find that the mindfulness seminars are helpful with that issue but will also raise your self-awareness beyond every day problem-solving to become a more emotionally intelligent person. It is a useful tool in every facet of your life."

A public relations person added:

"I guarantee that everyone will get something out of the mindfulness sessions. Which part will vary from person to person. It gives us an opportunity to learn some things that will help us in both our professional and personal lives. I wish more people could incorporate this in their lives. We all need to recharge and re-center ourselves in life."

A person from the finance department commented:

"I did not know what to expect. But I have learned so much about myself since attending these sessions and trying to practice mindfulness at home and at work."

Self-Awareness Builds Compassion

By being a non-judgmental witness to the way we experience and live our lives, we come to accept who we are, and we begin to learn self-compassion. This is not an easy thing for many of us. Until we have some self-compassion, we cannot truly extend it to others. Our soothing utterances are simply a display for the gallery—our own and that of the audience.

The Vital Importance of Self-Awareness

Some people shy away from self-reflection claiming it is narcissistic preoccupation or it isn't really doing anything productive. They would rather be doing meaningful things. Therein lies an unfortunate misunderstanding. We tend to forget that the quality of everything we think and do is a function of the quality of our minds. If we are not prepared to strengthen and improve the quality of our minds by "cleaning out our transmitters," we will always be on an inferior wave length. Worse still—we will not even know it! We will engage poorly, perform poorly, and feel poorly.

Self-awareness is critical to personal growth. It is fundamental to our physical health as discussed in the chapter on the Mind and the Brain. It is essential with respect to our relationships. It augments our cognitive skills. It helps us manage our anxieties and reactions. It builds resilience. It improves our self-confidence and our compassion. It is a foundational building block to a healthy life and effective engagement and performance at work.

MINDFULNESS AND EMOTIONAL INTELLIGENCE

Anger is never without a reason, seldom a good one.
- Benjamin Franklin

Emotion and Intelligence at Work

In Chapter 4, we discussed The Mind and the Brain. We saw how the interplay between the thinking brain and the emotion generator, affects the way we handle our emotions. We noted that the amygdala, which activates raw emotion prior to thought, reacts swiftly, while the thinking brain takes time to catch up.

The interplay between our emotions and our ability to think things through, is the basis of our emotional intelligence (EI). Navigating life successfully is dependent on our ability to bring our intelligence to our emotions and our emotions to our intelligence — at the right time, in the right circumstances, and in the right way. What makes this challenging is not only the speed with which our emotions kick in, but also the fact that attached to our emotions are memories and response repertoires etched into our bodies and our brains.

EI Components and Mindfulness

Peter Salovey, the American social psychologist and current President of Yale University, developed the idea of emotional intelligence subsequently popularized by psychologist and journalist Daniel Goleman. Based on their work, key components of EI are cited as:

Knowing oneself. Having self-awareness. Being able to recognize feelings as they occur. Having a certain self-reflectiveness in the moment.

Having the ability to monitor one's reactions in the moment and not to be engulfed by identification — something we discussed in Chapter 2. Non-identification is the ability to separate our thoughts and our feelings; to set them apart from us as the experiencing subject and look at them objectively.

Managing our emotions appropriately. This means that when we experience worry, anger, rage, fear, and overwhelm, we must handle these emotions in a fitting manner. This does not mean to deny or repress them, but rather that we choose our responses thoughtfully. It means finding perspective, not being reactive, not retaliating with personal attacks, and not resorting to passive-aggressive behavior. It means not being impulsive and impetuous, but rather showing self-control and restraint.

Motivating ourselves by marshalling our emotions in the service of our goals. This means using our emotions such as commitment, excitement, loyalty, joy and devotion to get us to focus and pay attention to the goals we have set ourselves.

Recognizing the emotion in others. To recognize the emotion in others means a) that we are not caught up in our own emotions, and b) that we are paying attention, being mindful, open, and accepting. Our task is to recognize others' emotions and not to judge them.

Being able to experience and show empathy. With empathy, we feel with the other person, whereas with sympathy we feel for the other person. Feeling with the other person means we feel as the other person does walking in his or her shoes. Not ours! True empathy does not come easily. It takes mindful attention and listening.

Displaying social skills. This means the ability to have good relationships; to communicate well; to handle oneself well in awkward or challenging situations, and to be appropriate regarding what one says and does.

Emotions Make us Human

Just as our ability to reason makes us human, so do our emotions. Without emotions we would be cold, calculating, machines or worse still psychopaths. Empathy is at the roots of our morality and our ability to inter-relate. Emotions inspire us, motivate us, energize us, humor us, and bring out the wonder of our humanity. It is the inappropriate emotion and the impulsive behaviors and responses that get us into trouble, that hurt others, and that render us unprofessional. Mindfulness can come to the rescue! Mindfulness, by slowing down our conditioned reactions, improves our EI and our ability to relate and engage at all times, and in all circumstances.

EI at Delta Dental

Comment from a claims analyst:

"Mindfulness is a two-way street. Here's how I think about it. An emergency for you is not necessarily an emergency for me. We need to think before we ask others at work to turn from their work to help us. Now I am more careful to ask only for what I need and can't do for myself. This has two benefits. First, I can justify interrupting others because it's necessary. Also, I learn more if I do things for myself and am more resourceful."

Comment from a technical analyst:

"My definition of a bad day used to be if someone disagreed with me or I felt they were judging me. Now, I have learned to put that aside, not dwell on the negatives and to take each personal or situation as it comes. I can do that because I look at people differently. Now I observe what people are saying rather than judging their thoughts or jumping to conclusions. I observe how people are feeling about me or my opinions, and I accept their approach and try to get the most of our conversations."

Comment from the Director of Finance:

"I am more connected with what's on the inside of people. I am also more in tune with each of my actions and I stay more present. There is a half second, a place in your mind, before reacting. You have control of this half second. It makes a big difference."

NO-ONE GETS A CLEAN DECK OF CARDS

Vet Care

A few years ago, I was asked by a friend of mine to help a friend of his whose business was in deep trouble. The business was a veterinary clinic that included a 24 hour emergency center and surgery. The CEO and owner, Sally-Ann, an accomplished vet herself, had started the business twenty years previously. For many years it had been a huge success attracting many soon to become loyal clients. However, in the last five years, the company had steadily lost those clients and was now in financial difficulty.

Sally-Ann claimed to be relieved to have my insights and assistance. I spent several days on site learning about Sally-Ann and the culture. It was a dismal situation. Staff turnover was off the charts.

At its height, the company had employed thirty-five people. It was down to fifteen and battling to make payroll. People came and left on a weekly basis. Staff was unhappy, poorly paid, screamed at and generally undermined. They took their frustrations out on the clients by being sharp, off-hand and lacking in compassion. Sometimes both the clients and their animals left before being treated, both with their tails between their legs.

Due to cash flow constraints, the surgery often ran out of basic medicines. Newly graduated vets were hired, many straight out of veterinary school, who had minimal practical experience. The veterinary assistants were in many cases more capable than the young graduates. This created its own tensions.

There was continuous drama in the surgery. Pain medication frequently disappeared. Vets on call did not show-up. Sally-Ann was forever stepping in working long hours. On more than one occasion, a young vet fainted in the middle of an operation. Surgery errors were on the increase.

Sally-Ann herself, was tired and super-strained. She feigned to care for her people and did not realize that people saw that she was disingenuous. She was inclined to lecture to all and everyone — including me — and changed her mind about decisions regularly. Nepotism was rife as her daughter and son, both employed by the firm, were hopelessly incompetent. They were given perks and power which they flaunted brazenly.

For Sally-Ann, stories mattered more than facts. Favorites got away with all and everything. She loved long meetings where everything was processed to death. The decisions made at the meeting — if any — were usually dropped with no follow through plan. Sally-Ann would get ferociously angry in public — often in front of clients — and lecture people endlessly about their mistakes. However, there were no further consequences.

The worst part of it all was that Sally-Ann and her husband Jack, the CFO, regularly had public screaming matches. These were so loud and intense, one could hear them throughout the buildings.

Staff would leave work crying. Clients would leave before being seen. And Sally-Ann would scream some more.

Sally-Ann told me that her greatest strength was her self-awareness and her relationships with people. She said she loved animals more than anything, even more than people, and would do anything for them. She was sick and tired of the lazy, disengaged people who came to work for her thinking they could have an easy ride. Whew!

What had happened to this friendly, warm, animal-centered family business? What had happened to Sally-Ann and her husband Jack? What had happened to loving attention, compassion and dedication? What new reality had hit this system?

I knew that some new reality, somewhere, somehow had triggered Sally-Ann and her company. It did not take me long to find out. Seven years prior to this period, Sally-Ann and Jack had lost one of their children in a car accident. Jack had begun drinking and gambling, using the company's money. Then two years ago, Sally-Ann had been diagnosed with intestinal cancer. She had bravely fought her way back after a life-challenging operation but remained in pain and dependent on heavy medication. It is understandable that this was more than the system could cope with. Fear of mortality was palpable everywhere.

I began private coaching with Sally-Ann and her daughter. I also held group sessions with her disengaged staff. We included mindfulness and meditation. The staff were relieved to get attention and to be appreciated. They were relieved to find some safety and regularity. They were relieved that Sally-Ann began to calm down. And they were relieved to sit, to pay attention to the present moment, to honor the silence. Their angers dissipated, and they came to focus on their love of the work, helping animals. They came to practice being in the present moment with the animals in distress. And they came to realize they were not victims of the system, but that they had their own inner strengths, their own values, and their own choices to make.

It was a long haul back. But it did turnaround. The animals are once again receiving the loving care to which Sally-Ann in her heart is so committed. Sally-Ann found relief too. She found a new resilience, and a new inner strength. Her fears subsided and so did her anger. She began *pranayama* (a Hindu breathing practice), went to yoga regularly and went for long walks in the forest—another place to get nature's healing touch. She reduced her medications and took up meditation. Jack quit being CFO and went for counseling. The incompetent children were encouraged to leave. The healing began.

RESILIENCE

In my experience, having worked as a consultant in the people business, for over thirty years, I have found that no-one gets a clean deck of cards. Whether it be in South Africa, England, Switzerland, Hong Kong, Hungary, India, or America, you name the place, no single life escapes some tough challenge, some sorrow, or some scar. That is life. There is no free pass.

One other thing I have learned, and I include myself in this observation, is that we all have far greater inner strength and resilience than we realize. There is an inner wholeness in each one of us, that when uncovered and appropriately touched or engaged, can perform the healing process from within. Sally-Ann, by taking time to turn inward, found her inner strength and her inner wholeness. Mindfulness and meditation are very powerful yet gentle and compassionate ways of stirring the embers of our dampened inner fires. The call to life and to live life fully is immensely powerful.

Resilience is our capacity to adapt to stressful circumstances. It is our ability to bounce-back in the face of shock, disappointment or loss. It is an ability not to become victim to circumstances or to give-in to the hard knocks of life.

Psychologists and neuroscientists have been carrying out all kinds of research to find out why some people are more resilient than others, and what kinds of innate strengths or circumstances build resilience.

They have found that a strong sense of self-awareness and self-understanding is one of the key ingredients of resilience. Being able to manage one's perceptions and one's emotions is also a great contributor.

People with a strong internal locus of control—they believe in themselves and their ability to shape their destiny—have greater resilience than others.

The famous MBSR program, which has run for almost forty years and where thousands of people have benefitted, confirms that meditation builds resilience.

To adapt and be effective in our topsy-turvy world, we need to build our resilience.

We need to roll with the punches, and treat challenges as learning opportunities. We need that inner strength, that inner shrine, to give us our center.

THE CHALLENGE OF ENGAGEMENT

In many organizations, workplace disengagement is a major problem. Workplace disengagement not only affects the organization, but the health and well-being of the individual. Disengagement, burnout, and apathy increases stress and anxiety often causing depression that impacts not only work, but home life.

As we know, a disengaged workforce radically affects the performance of any business. Productivity decreases, customers are neglected, errors increase, initiative disappears, communication degenerates, safety becomes a problem, and creativity declines. Based on the reports and on discussions with several disgruntled employees in disparate firms, a large percentage of those who are disaffected blame their bosses. Addressing these challenges, is the work of both the individual and the organization together, in mutual engagement and commitment, and with mutual accountability.

By taking a mindfulness perspective, tackling the employee engagement matter requires self-responsibility and self-accountability by all parties. As I have pointed out, an important aspect of mindfulness is that we take responsibility for our own experiences. This does not deny or repudiate the fact that at times our experiences will be distressing or unconstructive. Of course, we need to remove ourselves from abusive or unjust situations. What is important is that we have truly done our part to take responsibility for our perceptions, assumptions, biases, and filters. We have looked at our own stimulus-response mechanisms and our habitual reactions to having our needs filled, our desires met, and our dislikes eradicated. Otherwise, as the saying goes—whatever you run from will simply be waiting for you at the next corner.

MANAGING OUR MOST STRATEGIC RESOURCE

Brain Child

While I was growing up, my mother would talk about the rapidly changing nature of the world and how I would need to be adaptable. According to her, this would take an agile and resilient brain that could master thinking and ideas rather than techniques, as they are soon outdated. Developing Annabel's healthy and energetic brain was a major family project.

As discussed in the Introduction, besides my father's admonitions about it all being in the mind, I was endlessly "re-minded" to use my brain and my intellect wisely. My mother was determined I would have a healthy brain, so liver and sheep's brains were a regular repast. Why sheep's brains, of all things, are good for the brain, I have yet to fathom.

My father would studiously observe my activities. He would query what I was engaged in at various times of the day, and would comment. Working for many hours at a stretch was hard on the brain. Not eating properly starved the brain. Listening to music with earphones was harmful to the brain. Studying at night was tiring for the brain. Trying to do too many things at once depleted the brain. So it would go on.

My father had surely written the manual on brain optimization. I came to learn from him that the brain is a resource that needs to be taken care of and used strategically. When you are fresh, you do the difficult things. When you are tired, you rest, or you do the easy things. Doing complex work after a heavy meal, is a waste of time, as the brain is starved of blood which is tending to the digestion.

In between work, the brain needs little holidays and pick-me-ups. Holidays and pick-me-ups can be a few minutes of rest or meditation, a handful of nuts, maybe a small piece of good Swiss chocolate, sharing some jokes, breathing exercises in the fresh air, or doing something one enjoys doing that is not taxing — like reading an interesting article. But not on the computer!

I also learned that when I was mad or sad, I needed to change my mind. While I was working on that (it did not always come easily!), I should not engage in tasks that required carefully thinking or decision making. I should rather take a walk, go for a swim or play a game of tennis. My father had his tennis racquet ready at all times!

The brain is a marvelous organ, my father would say, use it well, and you can master anything. My father was way ahead of all the neuroscientists of today!

Brain Waves

I came to learn over the years that I am a morning person. I need to ensure that I have achieved my major goals for the day by 2 pm or 3 pm at the latest. After that, I slow down and am best at routine work or less intellectually challenging tasks.

Over the decade of developing my AI systems, I worked with hundreds of people and I noticed that their brain capacities responded to different rhythms too. People usually are fresh in the morning, so as a general rule, cognitively complex tasks should be tackled then. When people's brains are rested, they can prioritize, plan, deal with problems, set goals and so on. Routine functioning is handled best later in the day.

I also noticed that when people felt insecure, undermined or confused their decision-making was poor and inconsistent. They made errors, they were defensive, and they were lethargic and depressed. Fear, too, is a great inhibitor of brain effectiveness as shown in the following story:

The Fox, the Goose, and the Bag of Beans

One regular group exercise I sometimes use is to divide a large group of people into smaller units of threes and fours and then give them the following puzzle to solve. I tell them that they have a maximum of ten minutes to come up with a strategy for the farmer. And no — the goose cannot swim alongside the boat! I also tell them that after the exercise has been completed, each person will be asked to sing a few bars of their favorite tune in front of the entire group.

Exercise: A farmer went to market and bought a fox, a goose and a bag of beans. He set off home very happy with his purchases!

Getting home necessitated crossing a river. The only means of transport was a very small boat, too small in fact to carry more than the farmer, a man of fairly large proportions, and one of his purchases.

There was only one thing to do and that was to make several trips across the river. There was one complication however. Some of his purchases could not be left alone together.

The fox, if left alone with the goose, would make a meal of her. The goose could never resist devouring the beans. The poor farmer is faced with a dilemma.

Can you give the farmer advice of a strategy he could use to overcome his problem? Naturally he needs advice fairly quickly — faster than it takes to build a bridge across the water.

Constraints: All things have to travel in the boat.

As you can see, this is not a difficult exercise. But what I have found is that most groups cannot solve the problem within the time period, if at all!

Most recently, I tried the exercise with a group of twenty-four hi-tech engineers, most of whom had masters' degrees or doctorates in one of the STEM disciplines. I had divided them into six groups of four. At the end of the ten minutes, only one group out of the six cracked the simple puzzle.

You may have guessed the problem. The terror of singing publicly was on most people's minds. For the engineers, this was beyond frightening. Like my women in my finance class, a few of them ran to the bathroom instead of solving the puzzle.

Here is a very important reminder. Fear destroys our ability to think, be rational, to problem-solve, to make thoughtful decisions, and so on. Our thinking brain finds it very hard to stand-up to our fight-or-flight mechanisms. Any manager who forgets this dynamic is managing at his or her peril!

Brain Dance

The number of things we expect our poor brains to juggle each day is enormous. We are no longer sitting on our haunches in front of the hut admiring our harvests.

We are caught up from morning to night in a frenetic dance of brain juggling. Besides the turmoil of getting to work, there is the deluge of emails waiting for us like the "feed me" plant in the Little Shop of Horrors. Then there are meetings without end. In between we have our routine tasks. Then there are the tasks where we get paid to think. Here we initiate projects, we set goals, we prioritize, we define problems, we solve problems, we seek out information, we make decisions, and we dance around office politics. Then we do another dance at home.

The agility of the human brain is a wonder. We can switch wave lengths and respond to new events or information within seconds. Yet each switch takes energy, and assimilating brand new material takes a lot of energy. Dealing with the unknown takes even huger amounts of energy.

Managing with mindfulness means strategizing each day as to how we are going to accomplish our goals. We need to decide which tasks should be given to our brains at which times. Complex, cognitive juggling, such as priority setting, evaluating options, planning, dealing with an unstructured decision process, handling conflict, should all be tackled when we are fresh and only when we are fresh. Routine structured tasks can be assigned to times when the brain is less energized or when it needs a rest from heavy duty processing.

For example—Highly structured decisions like processing certain paperwork, or checking procedures have been followed, are good for the afternoon or evening.

Hiring employees is best either early in the morning or before noon. Leaving it until late in the afternoon is usually a mistake. Our bodies tend to be too tired to pick up subtle cues.

Difficult conversations are for first thing in the morning when we are fresh and have done some deep breathing to center us.

Highly unstructured decisions, such as planning, priority setting, defining problems and scoping their alternative solutions, are most definitely early morning tasks. Try not to leave this until the afternoon after you have been rendered brain dead by emails.

USING OUR BRAINS

We said managing ain't easy. It is one big juggling act. One has to manage oneself and manage others. One resource that is frequently not allocated in the most effective manner is or brains. Managing means using one's brains! Using one's brains in the most effective way possible. This means appreciating one's brain as one's most strategic resource. Each day should be prioritized as best as possible, where the most challenging tasks are tackled when the brain is fresh. Employees should be guided in doing the same.

A Reminder:
- The brain is an organ that needs care like any other
- The brain has a limited amount of energy which we need to use wisely
- Our brain is a strategic resource. It determines our daily functionality. We therefore need to use it consciously and resourcefully
- Long hours of uninterrupted work and what we call multitasking are tiring on the brain
- Brain pick-me-ups can serve as a break and can recharge the brain's energy
- Different people have different rhythms and the brain responds accordingly
- Work should be strategized around our rhythms

- Strong emotions, such as fear, affect our rationality and our decision-making effectiveness
- Humor is good for the brain
- We need to identify and anticipate brain drains, which includes people and events
- The mind is the greatest resource we have. We need to give it the attention it deserves. That is mindfulness

Chapter 9

Putting Mindfulness To Work—Part 1: Communication Strategies

THE AGE OF COMMUNICATION

In my consulting meanderings through countries and companies, I have yet to encounter an organization where people do not complain about the quality of communications. The irony is that we are living in the so-called communications age. We have more tools for better and faster communications than ever before. However, people complain communication is poor. They comment that if only communications would improve, the organization would save so much time and money.

Most people talk as if this is someone else's problem. Someone needs to fix communication! But who will take this on? Surely, it is everyone's responsibility.

Communication begins with each one of us. How do we communicate? What do we communicate? How do we pay attention? What is the quality of our listening? Do we listen to other people? Do we give them our undivided attention or just half-an-ear? Do we assume we know what someone is going to say before he or she says it? Do we even care about what he or she has to say? And then, how do we speak? Do we have meaningful things to contribute? Or do we just add to the noise? And of course reading and digesting information is another matter.

What about our meetings? Are they effective? Do the right things get communicated? And emailing? Do all those gazillions of emails communicate what truly needs to be communicated? Do people read carefully? Wherein lies the problem?

OUR LOST CONNECTION

Sound As Our Deepest Nature

Physicists describe the universe as a great ocean of pulsing, vibrating electromagnetic energy. Everything that exists is some form of this vibrating energy with various forms of density or vibrational frequencies. We are saturated with this energy, this light. At our atomic level, we are rhythmic pulsations in continuous vibration and movement. It is these vibrations that create sound.

Sound, is an important part of who we are. Eons ago, all sound held something magical, something special. It spoke to our connection to God, connection to the earth, connection to one another. In those olden days, when we lived a natural life, we were actively taught to listen to sounds — to the grass, to the wind, to the birds, and to our own souls. We can thus appreciate why chanting, and ritualized music or singing is used by many to attune themselves to the sacred or what to them is the Divine.

In our modern world, we have lost appreciation and reverence for sound. Our mental progress is marked by the development of the pre-frontal cortex that we discussed in Chapter 4. It is the executive mind that helps us think, analyze, evaluate, judge, and rationalize. The pre-frontal cortex helps us manage our animal instincts. In the process it has also turned many of our experiences into an abstraction. Sound is no longer about being attuned to ourselves and others in an embodied way as a deep sensation. Now we listen with our heads. We no longer appreciate that sound is the deepest resonance of who we are. Instead it has become a thought, not an experience.

We have also lost our ability to listen, to listen from within. We no longer know how to listen deeply. We listen for words and speak with words. These words have lost their connection to sound and vibration. We also talk and talk and talk without any real connection to what we are trying to convey. It is all head listening and head talk. We pay little attention to the idea of being harmonious.

MINDFUL LISTENING

> *Since in order to speak, one must first listen,*
> *Learn to speak by listening.*
> *- Rumi*

The Gift of Being Heard

I think we all agree that it is a great gift to be heard. We feel respected and appreciated when we are heard. Feeling heard is even more important than solving people's problems. They can do that best for themselves. People want to be heard — really heard and felt understood. Often, we feel we do not have time to put everything aside and give someone our undivided attention. Yet we cannot afford not to. Mindful listening is about giving that undivided attention.

With mindful listening, we are receptive to not only the words of the other, but to their sound, to their vibrations. We are listening not just with our ears, but with our entire beings. We are seeking attunement with the other. As we listen, it is not just the words we hear. We sense the emotion, the feelings, the significance of what is being conveyed.

With mindful listening, we clear our minds. We drop our egos that are dying to have their say. We push away our comparisons, biases, and judgments. We truly listen. We do not interrupt, play out opinions and scenarios in our minds, think of questions or rebuttals, look for what we do or do not want to hear, or let our minds finish sentences or rehearse what we are going to say next.

Mindful listening is honest listening. It is caring listening. It is carried out with an alert passivity. There is no strain, just openness. There is no anxiety, no need to control, and no need to influence the results. With relaxed attention, one hears a great deal. One gets a sense of the song behind the words. One hears what is both said and not said.

Listening is a search for understanding. With mindful attention, one understands — one stands under, or gets beneath the surface phenomenon. One truly hears. Once one truly hears, real communication has begun.

A Listening Exercise

Here is a mindful listening exercise that can be carried out between two people or with a group of people. The aim of the exercise is not to fall into the trap of being distracted or preoccupied, but to try to be in tune with what is being communicated at the deepest level.

This exercise also makes one more sensitive to improving one's own communication skills so that we may be heard. Here you are going to give your full moment to moment attention to another person with a non-judgmental mind. Every time your attention wanders away, you gently bring it back. You try not to think of other things, come up with a remark or rebuttal or advice, you just listen.

You listen with your entire body — not just your mind. You show through your body energetically that you are present and interested.

You can do this exercise formally or informally. Formally is where you make this mindfully listening exercise explicit. Here one person speaks, and another person listens in mindful silence. The informal practice is where you do not make your intention explicit but simply listen to someone and give them your mindful attention.

So now to the exercise — I suggest that people work in pairs. The first person tells the second person a story, or a problem, or a dream, or goal he or she wishes to achieve. It can be anything he or she feels comfortable with. The other person simply pays attention and listens. The speaker speaks for five uninterrupted minutes. The second person may only ask two clarifying questions at the end of the five minutes. Then he or she will thank the speaker and give feedback on what she or he heard — not the facts but the emotional content of the discussion. For example, I heard the joy or the sorrow or the confusion in your story. There may be no element of evaluation or assessment. There is simply a sharing of understanding. The feedback must be brief and non-judgmental. Remember the importance of body language.

The second speaker will then have his or her turn.

Rules for Listening
- Pay full attention
- Remember your body language
- Try not to evaluate, assess, second guess, compare, or judge what is being told
- Engage with your entire energy field — what are you seeing, sensing, tasting, touching?
- What energy vibrations are occurring between you and the speaker?
- Do not get caught up in asking questions
- Do not get carried away with agreeing, nodding, shaking your head, rolling your eyes
- Be calmly present — open, alert, attentive, interested, curious, engaged
- Pretend this is the last conversation you will ever have

After each speaker has had his or her turn, if this has been practiced within a group, the group can have a brief discussion on what the experience was like and what they learned.

MINDFUL SPEAKING
I will never forget my first day of PhD studies at Boston University. There were at least fifty students seated in the chapel of the Theology School eagerly awaiting to hear the opening remarks of the day.

A gowned professor took the stage and promptly launched into a long monologue on theology, study, commitments, ethics, expectations—you name it. In between, the professor would make some comment that I barely caught, after which he would roar with laughter. The rest of us dutifully laughed too. At the end of his tortuous presentation, another gowned professor went up to thank him. She said, and I will never forget these words: "Thank you Professor Confusion for a most profound and entertaining speech. It was so profound, I never understood a word!"

Boy—did we then roar!

One Conversation at a Time

So much of life is affected by the quality of our conversations. We build and break many relationships, one conversation at a time. If we are poor listeners, it is likely we are also poor speakers. Why? Because we are not there. We are not present, paying attention. We have not trained ourselves to make every moment count. Instead we fall into the motor-mouth trap. This is when we talk just for the sake of talking. We say nothing of any value. We simply make unconnected sounds. Someone talks, we talk back. No-one talks, we talk to fill the space.

Mindful speaking means being totally present in every way to everything we say. It is about consciously selecting your topic, your words, and your body language as you attentively convey your message. Your goal is to enhance engagement and connection. You are interested in advancing the relationship with the people with whom you are conversing. You want to give him or her something of value.

Mindful speaking is about being attuned to others and the situation. Mindful speaking is purposeful. It is about moving things forward. It is about progression. It is about creating new options, new perspectives and new ideas. Mindful speaking is about increasing harmony in the world. Mindful speaking avoids the temptation to engage in gossip, criticism and negative comments.

Mindful Speaking Tips

- When you speak, be totally present to what you wish to convey
- Be selective about your language. Sloppy speech reflects a sloppy mind
- Bear in mind your posture. A good posture makes mindful speaking easier
- Make your speech meaningful. Let every word count. Less is more
- You do not always have to speak. A nod or a warm smile will sometimes be far more meaningful
- Try to make each discussion open, accepting and uncritical. Drop gossip, slander, and negative comments. They never help anyone
- Make your speech harmonious. Remember it reflects your deepest source

The Six Rs of Speaking

Mindful speaking is saying the *right thing*, with the *right intention*, to the *right person/s*, in the *right way*, at the *right time*, for the *right duration*.

As you go about your day, at home, working alone in your office or cubicle, talking to a group, or attending a meeting, stay mindful. Listen and observe — yourself and others. Speak mindfully and observe — yourself and others. Mentally note how much you listened, truly listened, and whether what you said added value, real value. As you practice, you will find your energy improve and that you have found a few more hours each day!

MINDFUL READING

In his intense book, *The Shallows: What the Internet is Doing to our Brains*, Nicholas Carr documents how the increase in use of the internet is destroying, among other things, our memories and our ability to read.

He explains how the layout of the pages and the flashing of adver-
tisements, popups, side-bars and then the intermittent videos, have
ruined our ability to concentrate and to read effectively. He claims
that young people who spend a lot of time either on the computer, or
on their phones, have lost the ability to read and comprehend pas-
sages. He cites research into the comprehension skills of students at
a variety of ages. The picture is bleak. Younger and younger students,
attached to all their technical gadgets have minimal comprehension
skills, and can barely read one page accurately and then report on
what they have read.

As a former professor, I am very sad to say that this has been my
experience too. The younger people cannot only not read and comprehend, they cannot write. More recently I have received papers to
be graded that included the texting form of grammar and spelling
such as, "U r rite," or "All is A-OK." The students are then perplexed
why they do not receive As for their papers!

Reading with comprehension is an important communication skill.
As with all the things we have discussed, it is a matter of slowing
down and being present. Not rushing, not looking for the "gist," but
reading to understand. Besides, our emailing challenges which we
discuss the next chapter, reading those emails — the worthwhile
ones — with dedicated attention, will save a lot of time, and a lot of
further emailing, and a lot of unnecessary repetitive work.

This is simply a plea to pay a little more attention as you read
whatever email, newsletter, client letter of complaint or praise, policy
document, and so on. Carr warns us that if we do not practice our
auditory memory and reading skills, we will lose them. So use
them — or lose them.

MINDFUL MEETINGS

Another Blasted Meeting!
Talk to many people and they will say they spend their lives in meetings. Each day they go from one blasted meeting to the next.

In attempts to improve communications, many organizations have increased the number of meetings. Despite these many get-togethers, frustration reigns. People invariably complain that most meetings are unproductive and a waste of time. They remain being confused, misaligned, misdirected, or lacking the information they need to be effective in their jobs.

Some say that meeting preparation is inadequate, meeting execution is poor, and meeting follow-up is mostly non-existent or mediocre at best. People often joke about the meeting after the meeting.

One client I worked with had a real problem with the meetings of his senior management team. People dreaded the meetings, often arriving late and armed with all kinds of strategies as to how to get through the laborious two hours.

One VP slept through every meeting. He would arrive, take up is usual seat and within five to ten minutes be sound asleep. The other VPs would time how long he slept. Another VP would — ostensibly taking notes — plan her overseas vacations. A third VP would send emails. The VP of HR would review job applications. The VP of Operations would read articles for his online MBA program.

The CEO, who knew what was going on, would simply continue with the meeting. Now and again he would ask questions of various people who would feign attention and give some non-committal response. Two, sometimes three hours later, everyone would emerge tired and disengaged to see what real work they might accomplish.

Nowadays many people arrive at meetings with their laptops and their phones, ostensibly to write notes or to be sure to be in touch for that all-important customer call. Well, let's face it. That is baloney! The technical crutches are there to help with their indifference, boredom, need for distraction, and attempt at multitasking. How many people email during meetings? Or keep sneaking a peak at what is posted on Facebook? Or worse still, look at vacation packages?

There is no doubt that in most organizations the investment in meeting time is enormous. The question is: What is the return — if anything — on those investments?

The Purpose of Meetings

All meetings should have an explicit, articulated, and communicated purpose. This could include:

- To gather information
- To disseminate information
- To formulate vision, strategy, priorities, or goals
- To decide on policies, projects or initiatives
- To align people around strategies, projects, initiatives, and goals
- To check on goal progress
- To address people issues
- To allocate resources
- To handle ad hoc decisions, unexpected events, or crises
- Some combination of the above

The purpose of the meeting needs to be clearly identified and communicated in advance. Mental clarity is required to set meeting objectives and to craft an agenda that elicits the desired outcomes after the meeting. Desired outcomes need to be carefully articulated and communicated as needed meeting take-aways.

Running Meetings

Everyone invited to the meeting should have the agenda and stated purpose well in advance. They should also know the expected outcomes of the meeting. People should be informed that attention and presence are required. Laptops and cell phones should not be permitted except for the designated note taker.

Attendees should be reminded of the importance of mindful listening. Even if people are discussing matters that may not seem to concern certain individuals directly, the meeting facilitator should remind them that everything has some impact on everyone, as the organization is an integrated system. The more one knows and takes an interest in everything that is going on now, the more effective a contributor each person will be.

Transitioning

As part of mindfulness training, I encourage everyone to practice mindful transitioning. This means that every time one physically or mentally moves into a new space or a different type of work setting, such as a meeting, one should take a moment and make the transition conscious. This means putting down what one is presently doing and allowing some space to prepare for the next interaction. This can be done by stretching, deep breathing for a minute or two, consciously clearing one's mind and acknowledging the new encounter, or looking out of the window and breathing in the sky.

Mindful transitioning can truly make a big difference to being present. These actions are intended to awaken one's consciousness to the transition. To get one inside one's body. To clear and refresh the mind, and to invite one's intention to be attentive and present.

Attending Meetings—What Mindset Will You Bring?

From a mindfulness perspective, we take personal responsibility for our experiences. We acknowledge that the way we perceive things determines the quality of our lives.

For every disappointing, dysfunctional, wasted meeting, we know that some of the responsibility is ours. Knowing this, it makes sense that we attend meetings with the right attitude and wanting to make a positive contribution. This begins of course with our commitment to be attentive and present. We also practice mindful listening and speaking.

One CEO I work with is adamant about having people's conscious attention at her meetings. No-one may bring any technological device to the meeting. Each meeting begins with two minutes of silence to allow for transitioning. Meetings end with another two minutes of silence to allow for gratitude and respect for everyone who attended the meeting.

If she notices anyone not paying attention during the meeting—and I have observed her in action—she calls the meeting to an immediate halt. She asks people whether they wish to be present and work on the meeting agenda with attention or commitment or not. With a sharp eye given to the distractors, the meeting invariably moves on at a lively pace. At some point, to soften the tone, she usually makes some humorous remark about distractions and lagging attention. People love her meetings and laugh respectfully at her "sharp eye."

Ending Meetings

In my experience meetings that exceed ninety minutes are wasteful. People cannot truly stay alert and attentive for a longer time frame. A well-thought-through agenda with a clearly-defined purpose and needed outcomes, along with a well-run meeting where people are attentive and on task, rarely requires more than one hour or ninety minutes to achieve its declared goals.

Meetings need to begin on time and end on time. Within twenty-four to forty-eight hours thereafter, everyone should receive the minutes of the meeting plus a reminder for their individual follow-up responsibility. Everyone who attended the meeting should be tasked with at least one responsibility. The mindfulness test will be how well one remembers all the details of the meeting without referring to the minutes and the follow up notes.

After the meeting, many people say "did we discuss that?" or "I don't remember that decision?" Well, who was not paying attention?

MINDFUL EMAILING

That Thing We Love to Hate!

People love to complain about the number of emails they receive and the state of their inbox. Many of us assume that we must read both the welcome and unwelcome intruders and respond to them. We also use some of our most valuable time, when we are fresh and have energy, to tackle the email onslaught.

Responding to emails can be a great distraction from tackling other challenging work like meeting goals, finishing projects, engaging with customers, having difficult conversations with staff members, finding creative solutions to problems, initiating new projects, and being seen by employees. Hiding behind emails often provides a marvelous excuse. Let's be honest!

Suggested Email Exercise

Select one day in which you will review your emails—both sent and received. Select a good chunk of them and then analyze their contents.

- How many are repeats due to incorrect or missing information?
- How many could have been condensed into one email instead of sending two or three or five?
- How many include inaccurate, missing, or misleading information?
- How many are not really intended for you?
- How many are just inane chit chat that served as a distraction from real work?
- How many are part of the "copy all" chain?
- How many might you just not answer and there will be no consequence?
- What percentage of those emails were real work, efficiently communicated?

Email Mindset

As with everything we have discussed so far, the most important thing about doing anything—anything at all—is our mindset. What quality of mind are we bringing to our thoughts and our actions?

If we "hate" emails, they will get the better of us. We will write thoughtless emails and perpetuate the ineffective, unwelcome chain.

If, on the other hand, we recognize they are to be managed like any resource, we will take control and develop a strategy.

General Email Strategies

- Do not to look at your email five seconds after you wake up. If you do, your day of distractions will have begun
- Have an arrangement with the key people in your life and at work that important messages or communication will be made by phone
- Organize your day around email responses as if they were meetings, i.e. have email meeting times. Stick to them unless something exceptional comes up
- Do not exceed one hour for each email meeting
- Try to limit your email meetings to a maximum of three hours spread over the day
- Do not use the first hours at work for emails unless they are needed specifically for a project or to commandeer people to meet some goals
- Ensure that you unsubscribe from all the advertising, Facebook reminders, and other garbage that finds its way into your inbox
- Tackle the most important and significant emails first. Try not to fire off emails in the sequence in which you have received them
- Clarify with the people you work with which emails you need to be copied on. Sometimes it takes five or six emails to get a meeting scheduled. So, you receive the back and forth of everyone's response as to availability. What a waste of time! Appoint one person responsible for coordinating the times
- Limit using the "reply all" button. Think carefully when you use it as to whether ALL need to know every little detail
- Do not email and speak to others at the same time or while eating lunch
- Ignore emails that do not command action
- Limit the *"thank you, have a great weekend, how was your weekend? I must tell you about Fred"* emails. Keep that for after hours—your time, your email, your text

Mindful Emailing

Emailing is communication. It has become a very important way of communicating. Just like mindful listening and mindful speaking, it should be carried out with mindfulness.

- Mindful emailing requires us to be attentive and present. We are writing to this person thoughtfully and with the intention to engage in a constructive manner
- We should repeatedly remind ourselves that the way in which we email reflects the communication culture of the organization
- Our emails should not be "me-mails"—all about us, what we need, when and how. Rather the email is a communication about how together we are engaged in something constructive for the organization
- Emails have an impact on others. We need to show care for the receiver. It is our cyber footprint. While it can be relegated to Trash, it may not be erased in the mind of the receiver that easily
- A little courtesy goes a long way. How about including people's names and a thank you when appropriate?
- Mindful emails do not include emotive or negative comments as part of their content. We are email environmentalists. We do not throw our trash into the environment. We do not pollute people's sensitivity by being hasty, thoughtless, rushed, distracted, and forgetful
- If you are not in a good place about something, and an email triggers certain distress, take time before you respond. Breathe. Stretch. Take a walk. Look at the sky. Get perspective. Think of the last good joke you heard. Dis-identify—do not make it personal even if it seems that way. At best, pick up the phone and have a mindful conversation
- Remember, mindfulness is about slowing down stimulus-response. Try to become a strategic emailer. Someone whose emails are on task, advance progress on real

problems, and are a pleasure to read. You will make a great contribution to the organization if you can role model leadership in this way

Chapter 10

Putting Mindfulness To Work—Part 2: Performance Strategies

WHAT WE CALL "WORK"

In this chapter, I address several critical activities that relate to organizational performance. Obviously, there are many more activities than the ones outlined. My purpose is to illustrate how mindfulness can play a vital role in advancing the organization's vision, effectiveness and creativity.

ORGANIZATIONAL VISION DEPENDS ON ATTENTION

Everything is Interdependent

In 2004, a massive tsunami hit the northern tip of Sumatra on the Banda Aceh coast. More than 250,000 people died. Scientists were astounded at the tsunami's size and the force. How had they not seen or predicted this?

Get this—Months after the event, it was reported that the animals had fled the shores days before the tsunami hit! Their losses were minimal. But nobody had been paying attention!

Realistic Visions

Without doubt, an organization needs a realistic, compelling vision to survive. The key point here is the word "realistic." How does one define the word realistic?

Let us begin with the word "vision." Vision refers to being able to see. To see also means to understand. Vision refers to understanding. We use "vision" in business when referring to a statement that guides courses of action for the future based on some kind of understanding.

A realistic vision is an idea of the future based on a deep and clear understanding of what is unfolding in the present. The present foretells the future. This brings us to mindfulness. By being mindful, we are attentive, present, in sync, in tune with the current situation — whatever that may be — as it is unfolding. We read the tea leaves for what is currently being shown. We observe the animals leaving the shore! There are no fortune tellers. Seeing the future requires being wholly attentive to the present.

Let us turn to the word "realistic." Realistic vision statements or guiding principles are based on reality. Reality refers to what is actually occurring. It is things as they actually exist. Realistic vision statements are not wish-fulfilments, ego-driven desires, or distractions from business challenges — which regrettably many vision statements tend to be. A realistic vision is one that anticipates the future based on what is happening now. Truly understanding what is happening now requires the quality of attention that we refer to as mindfulness.

THE IMPORTANCE OF GOALS

Goal Setting

If you ask people what their goals are, many will list their tasks. If you ask senior management whether they have a clearly defined hierarchy of goals that aligns employees' mindsets and performance requirements, most will mention what they are personally being measured on, and will possibly name their own contribution to the organization's goals.

I have found few organizations that can show a chart that outlines everyone's goals and how those goals support those of the next person in the hierarchy. Although people throw around the term SMART goals, in my experience, many still do not know how to implement them or how to make them part of the corporate culture.

I have helped many organizations implement goal measurement and reporting systems and I have taught seminars on goal setting. I have learned along the way that it is a mistake to assume that people automatically understand what a goal is, how to establish a realistic one, and how to measure achievement. They understandably need help, as this is not an easy process.

Achieving Goals

Either as individuals, or as organizations, we are not that good at achieving our goals. This is understandable in the face of new realities where we have had to reorient or refine those goals. However, many of the goals we miss are for other reasons. These reasons include:

- Unrealistic goals to start with
- No real way to measure progress on the goals
- Conflicting goals which no-one mediates or prioritizes.
- Lack of will and self-discipline
- A poor understanding of how our unconscious challenges or sabotages our ability to achieve our goals
- Poor prioritization of tasks so that goals are met on time
- Receiving orders from our supervisors to keep changing our goals
- No recognition for having achieved previous goals so why bother this time
- A culture that does not organize around goals and their attainment
- Digital distractions which are an increasing problem

Digital Distractions

According to digital marketing company, Smart Insights, on average people download 30 apps per month and spend 87 hours per month internet browsing via their smartphones. Based on these numbers, the equivalent of two working weeks of more than 40 hours each are devoted to browsing the internet! Research also shows that people spend an average of just three to five minutes at their computer working on the task at hand before switching to Facebook or another website, or to an app on their phones.

Using fMRI (functional magnetic resonance imaging) to measure brain activity, neuroscientists have found that ignoring distractions takes significant mental effort. If our executive friend, the pre-frontal cortex, is taken up with resisting distractions, it has less capacity to complete important work tasks, write progress reports, develop sales projections, or push through on other goals it is supposed to be working toward. It is also soon exhausted and not fresh enough to tackle essential tasks.

The constant competition for our attention means that we engage in continuous partial attention. We don't get our minds deeply into any one task or topic. We do our multitasking thing which is a misplaced survival strategy. As individuals, and from an organizational perspective, there is a huge price to pay.

At the personal level, we are literally diminishing the capacity of our minds. At the organizational level, we are destroying the creative resources of the firm on which its survival depends.

How Mindfulness Helps with Goals
- By being more present and attentive, we are likely to set more realistic goals
- By being less anxious and stressed, we can slow down and deal better with conflicting priorities
- Mindfulness and meditation improves self-discipline and the ability to focus our minds. It helps us fend off distractions
- We are less dependent on other's approval as determinants of our performance. We achieve each goal for its own sake

- Through heightened self-awareness, we are more in touch with our unconscious fears, biases, desires, and inner baggage that might inhibit achieving our goals
- Our heightened attention to the present enables us to be motivated and engaged with what it is we are accomplishing. We are less in the mechanical world of performing tasks in a habitual, non-conscious manner

DECISION-MAKING

While developing my AI systems, I learned a fair deal about decision-making. I learned that we can analyze decisions very rationally after the fact, but many decisions, when made are not always totally rational. We make the decision and then find the rationalizations afterwards. This is not necessarily a negative thing. In fact, many of our better decisions might be based on intuition or emotion. However, there is some validity in looking at our decision-making and understanding what ingredients lead to the most effective decisions.

Important Decision-Making Ingredients

We can say that effective decision-making requires critical thinking which is the clear testing of assumptions, biases, and hidden expectations. It also requires an ability to cut through uncertainties and ambiguities.

We can say further, that decision-makers need to be able to distinguish between problems and issues. They need to work with incomplete, and often mixed and confusing information. They need to know what they don't know in as far as possible. They should be prepared to invite people to the discussion who have very contrary ideas to their own.

Effective decision-making should also provide the path for effective execution. It should include plans for mindful communication to harness engagement and gain commitment. Many decisions are made without a detailed plan for follow through resulting in a massive floundering of confused action.

Steps in Decision-Making

Decision-making comprises several steps. While these are listed below in sequence, most often they occur in a circular or iterative manner. An important thing to bear in mind is that where one begins in defining the problem, determines where one ends up.

One of the unconscious habits of many people is to see all problems through the same lens. For example, all problems are seen to stem from incompetence, or competition, or power dynamics, or the need to be more productive... and so on. Experts can readily fall into this trap. This is one good reason to get more than one opinion when framing a problem.

The decision-making process usually includes the following:

- Identification of a problem
- Identification of missing information or knowledge
- Framing of the problem
- Specification of what solving the problem achieves, i.e. the objectives
- Identification of ethical issues and the ethical values that will inform the decision-making process
- Determination of the criteria for solving the problem
- Generation of alternative approaches to solving the problem
- Consideration of uncertainties that may affect the problem definition or solution
- Consideration of the consequences for each problem solution
- Identification where possible of unintended consequences
- Review of the trade-offs
- Consideration of the risks and one's own risk tolerance
- Revisiting of the framing of the problem, the ethical considerations, and the consequences

How Mindfulness Helps Decision-Making

By now many of the attributes of mindfulness will be familiar to you. As a reminder, here are some of the ways that mindfulness helps improve the quality of our decisions.

Mindfulness also helps us be aware of and manage our fears so that they do not cloud our judgment. Remember the fox, the goose and the bag of beans in Chapter 8.

Of course, it begins with being more calm and focused. Our reactive tendencies have been tempered so we allow some time for reflection between stimulus and response. This also allows for more options.

With mindfulness, we are more attentive, more focused and are able to remain more concentrated in the face of competing claims and distractions. Because of a better integration of thought and emotion, as we discussed in Chapter 8 under EI, we can decide more wisely to what extent emotion should play a role in a decision. Mindfulness also promotes confidence and creativity, which is something we explore a little later in this chapter.

PERFORMANCE

Outsourcing Our Minds

It seems with our love of technology that we are not just outsourcing jobs, but outsourcing our minds. Smartphones, apps, continuous posting on Facebook, and the downloading of marketing distractions keeps us from having to concentrate our way through challenging problems, perform critical thinking, and adapt to new behaviors.

As reported recently in Mindful magazine, in 2014 an experiment was carried out where smartphones where briefly taken away from a group of people. This group was so distressed that they opted for receiving electric shocks rather than being alone without their phones and left with their thoughts.

It is totally ironic, but we have now hundreds of mindfulness apps to remind us and to help us be mindful. The whole idea of mindfulness is to strengthen our capacity to do these things for ourselves! We also have soothing words and music to help us meditate. But the real power of meditation lies in us getting to know ourselves in silence.

We can now buy mindful games and cards to help mindfulness become an enjoyable activity. It seems we have left nothing, or little, to our will, our conscious intention, self-discipline, and the marvelous capacities of our minds. We have turned everything into an immediate gratification, problem-solving, discomfort-removing, technical gadget. Sadly, we do not realize we are destroying our minds. And our minds are our greatest power and resource.

Productivity — I Did It!

How often do we say: "I had a productive day!"? This could be after a day working at home or work. On those days don't we feel good? Don't we feel that the day was worthwhile, purposeful, fun, engaging? Don't we feel proud of ourselves, smart, and valuable? Don't we feel a little exhilarated? Don't we wish that everyday were like that?

Usually those productive days did not just happen on their own. They came together due to a number of factors. Such as:
- For some reason, we were motivated to set our own agenda
- We were intentional, focused, undistracted, and purposeful
- We set clear boundaries with others — "Not now, I am busy!"
- Maybe we organized ourselves well in advance
- We were in the right frame of mind. We could concentrate and be totally present
- We felt good — not overly stressed or anxious — just determined
- We felt effective, in command and personally valuable

On those productive days, we know we were working on things that matter in the best way that we could. We were goal driven. If only many more days were like that! Mindfulness adds to those productive days.

Productivity — What to Focus On

I remain surprised how few organizations stress the difference between effectiveness and efficiency. Effectiveness refers to doing the right things, the right way. It is doing those things that advance the mission, vision, and goals of the organization. Efficiency refers to getting things done in the fastest or most cost-effective manner. We can thus be efficient but not effective.

Alas, many employees are proud of how efficient they are but do not realize, and are not given the timely feedback, that they are not prioritizing and working on the things that really matter. They are well-meaning but essentially ineffective.

Worse still, for employees and organizations alike, many people measure their performance by the number of hours they have spent at work. To them this demonstrates their commitment and their dedication. They tend to forget—it is not input that counts, but the quality of output of the right things! Clearing the email inbox is not a measure of effective performance.

Productive people focus on accomplishments. They are goal oriented. They demonstrate quality attention and an ability to stay the course. They can fend off distractions and select the right things to work on amidst the tumult of competing information and conflicting demands.

Mindfulness plays a constructive role here. Neuroscience research reports that people who meditate regularly are better at focusing when assailed with multiple distractions. They are also better able to hold a goal in mind and not be deterred when there are competing and conflicting demands.

Organizations depend on productive people who are effective. Mindfulness helps as we see in the stories below.

Mindfulness and Productivity at Delta Dental

The following are comments from Delta Dental employees who have been attending the Mindfulness sessions.

A professional relations staff member commented on the impact of the mindfulness sessions at Delta Dental as follows:

"For example, the call center and claims departments have daily goals for us in how many calls to take and claims to process. You could get stressed about making your numbers, but in discussions with my colleagues I tell everyone to take one call at a time, do their best and don't worry about the numbers. Think about being present or just think about one thing at a time. Stay focused on the caller (or the claim) and everything will work out. You'll do a good job on the call/claim and make the numbers."

She continued, "I want to feel good about how I am doing my job. Mindfulness has helped. It helped me change my attitude. It helped me listen with an open mind, so I could enjoy the calls and letters more. It taught me to take a deep breathe between calls to get set and in the right frame of mind to respond as I should. I now feel good about how I do the work and about my job. Each call is different. You don't know what to expect. Some people are pleasant, and some people are unhappy. So you have to put yourself in their position, and mindfulness helps to do that and to be more compassionate and respond appropriately to each one. I have to be ready to respond to each person's attitude and have the right attitude for them."

"I find that I accomplish more every day. It's about applying mindfulness to my co-workers as well as our clients. I enjoy my work more and I'm more productive. Yes, it's possible to enjoy work more and accomplish more with less frustration or struggle if you are mindful. For example, I recently finished seven appeal response letters that my manager said were good and needed very few corrections. I know that being mindful helped me write those letters as they should be written."

A claims analyst reported "I've reduced the "roller-coaster" work effect that I have allowed in the past for as long as I can remember. For instance, while training someone or overseeing their work I make it a point to ask them to collect all their questions for review at a specific time that works for us all.

I know that I'm focusing on the work I need to do (as defined by my department's priorities), rather than allowing myself to be distracted by small interruptions. For example, I only check my email two times a day now, so I have fewer distractions and can focus on what's important. The only exceptions are when an email is an emergency or when I have to balance the need to respond to another department's requests. I am more conscious of performing well on the right things."

A systems analyst said: "I try not to live the future. That doesn't mean I don't plan—because planning is important. What I means is that I don't waste time imagining scenarios that don't happen. For example, a project is due in one week and I spend time thinking about all that could go wrong in the testing and fear the deadline may not be met. This is a possible scenario but it may play out very differently. So, now I focus on what needs to be done and do not waste time on the 'what ifs,' I focus on performing and getting my job done."

An IT Coordinator related the following: "I used to do a lot of things at work but wasn't sure what they accomplished at the end of the day. Now I know what I've accomplished, and I am someone who appreciates attaining objective outcomes so I use mindfulness as a tool to achieve real progress. I get a lot more done without multitasking. It's a lot easier to do a good job on what I'm working on when I'm focusing only on that task. There is value in taking the time to slow down and do each task well, rather than 'getting the job done' only to have to repeat it or deliver something that is low quality."

FROM MULTITASKING TO UNITASKING

Due to massive information overload and the high pressure to get things done, many employees survive daily on the "got it off my list!" mantra. The approach taken to diminish the never-ending lists is to engage in a frenzy of multitasking. As a result, the quality of what gets done gets lost in the mania to reduce the ever-growing catalog of to-dos, emails, and projects required to rectify previous projects.

By now everyone knows that multitasking is a total fallacy. The mind is not a computer with several processors that can process things in parallel. We have only one processor and one attention band. Our transmitters can only receive and send on one wavelength at a time.

When multitasking, we are actually snatching and switching our attention from one item to the next. Because we do not stop and plan and prioritize our burgeoning to-do list, we madly try to do everything at once—or so we tell ourselves—and are thus ineffective, inaccurate, unfocused, and uncreative. We become masters at the diddley-squat and pat ourselves on the back for having survived another day.

With mindfulness, multitasking is out, and unitasking is in! Tom found us this new word that is now part of the English lexicon. Unitasking is doing one thing at a time. With mindfulness, we change the culture from multitasking to unitasking.

The lists no longer control us, we control the lists. With focus, goal setting, emphasis on what is most effective to do, we rapidly purge our lists of many of the unnecessary or unimportant tasks we might delete or delegate.

CREATIVITY AND FLOW

"If you want to draw a bird, you must become a bird."
- Hokusai (Japanese artist)

All organizations, regardless of size, industry or stage in the life cycle, are dependent on the creativity of their workforce. It is creativity that keeps the organization alive and adaptive to changing realities. It is creativity through new ideas and new practical innovations that enables the organization to create new products, new services, and new revenue streams. It is creativity that attracts new blood, and gives employees opportunities to flourish and grow. It is creativity that shapes the culture. It is through creativity that the organization can make its meaningful contribution to society.

The Google Effect

How often and how quickly do we turn to Google when we cannot remember a name or a fact? Frequently and within seconds—right? This is now referred to as the LMGT (let me Google that) trap.

Psychologist Larry Rosen, who researches the cognitive effects of digital technology, reports that we forget very quickly things we look up. Straining to remember them, strengthens our retrieval mechanisms and builds the neuron connections that improve our memories. By looking things up on Google, instead of straining to recall them from memory, we do not remember them going forward and we become more dependent on looking things up in the future.

Further, the less facts and information accessible to our conscious minds (sitting in memory), the less creative we are. New ideas come from novel combinations of disparate, seemingly unrelated facts and elements. The more of these knocking around in our brains, the more possible combinations there are, and the more chances for the generation of creative ideas. Google robs us of our own creativity!

We Are All Creative

Many people claim they are not creative, that they are better at executing. This is unlikely to be true. We are all innately creative. As children, we could make trucks out of twigs, palaces out of sand, animals out of stone, and dresses out of wrapping paper. There was no end to our ideas. Over the years, maybe we were ridiculed or pressed to be rational and pragmatic, so we buried our creativity in the bottom drawer of our souls. However, the soul survives on creativity and expression. She is always waiting for an opportunity to express herself. When she does, we feel excited, engaged, and alive. Mindfulness feeds the soul.

A Climate of Creativity: Turning Work into Flow

A mindfulness culture is one fertile for creativity. Here, as discussed repeatedly, people are encouraged to live in the present moment. In so doing, they become absorbed in whatever they do. They drop their ego defenses, they forget themselves, they stop editing, evaluating, selecting, rejecting, and judging everything. They are immersed, fascinated, absorbed in the present.

It is in this environment, Mihaly Csikszentmihalyi, the author of *Flow*, wrote that we experience flow. Sometimes we refer to it as the zone. There is a sense of exhilaration, a deep sense of enjoyment.

During these times, nothing else seems to matter. Our attention does not waver. There are no distractions. We are all there in a flow of consciousness, energy and movement. We are so involved in our activity that everything seems spontaneous and automatic. Often there is an experience of wonder and awe as things come together in marvelously inexplicable ways. There is a transcendence of the self and the experience of bliss, of rapture, and of exaltation. Through our attention and presence, with open-mindedness and open-heartedness, we feel at one with the world.

Every organization is dependent on the creative energies of its people wanting to, in some way or another, to be expressed. Mindfulness enables us to return to the innocence we had as small children totally taken up in the present moment of our wondrous creativity. It is here where we can see that work — whatever it is — is divine play!

Chapter 11

Mindfulness: A Better Me; A Better You; A Better World

"I have come to the frightening conclusion
that I am the decisive element.
It is my personal approach that creates the climate.
It is my daily mood that makes the weather.
I possess tremendous power to make life miserable or joyous.
I can be a tool of torture or an instrument of inspiration.
I can humiliate or humor, hurt or heal.
In all situations, it is my response that decides whether a crisis is
escalated or de-escalated,
and a person humanized or de-humanized.
If we treat people as they are, we make them worse.
If we treat people as they ought to be,
We help them become what they are capable of becoming."
        - Johann Wolfgang von Goethe

THIS BOOK IS ABOUT MINDFULNESS

This book is about mindfulness. It is about adopting a new way of being. You could say, adopting a new approach to life.

This new way of being, is about changing our minds. Changing our minds about what we are going to give attention to and how. Changing our minds on where we are going to place our focus, our effort, our energy, our emotion, our vitality and our love. In fact, changing our minds affects everything. It changes our lives. By doing so, it changes the lives of others.

Adopting mindfulness as a way of being in the world by intentionally paying loving attention to the present moment, non-judgmentally, changes us physically, emotionally, and cognitively. It revitalizes our brains, and changes our neural connections. We are in better control of our emotions in a way that gives us more freedom, more composure, and less anxiety and stress. We find that we think more clearly, focus better, and dedicate ourselves to our tasks with greater concentration and clarity.

Changing our minds requires some effort and commitment. We need to earnestly want to live a more relaxed, poised, and effective life. We need to want to be accountable for our actions, have better perspective, be less reactive, and find an inner freedom. We need to want to live out of the fullness of our potential, and be able to find value in each moment.

We need to want to show up differently where we are present, and our presence is a present to others. We need to want to be a better father, mother, daughter, son, employee, manager, lover, and friend.

These are some of the benefits of mindfulness. The extent to which we experience them is entirely up to us! This is one place where we have full control. We make up our mind how we are going to perceive, think, evaluate, decide, and react. It is all up to us. The ball of life is squarely in our court.

While this seems daunting—and it is because we are unaccustomed to this way of being in the world—we will find that we have inner resources to help us that we never imagined. We are on a new journey. Every step counts—no matter how small or how big. The more we engage in this process for the love of it—for the love of shaping our own becoming—the more we will blossom into its benefits.

THE POWER OF ATTENTION

We are all gifted with a very powerful awareness technique and that is the power of attention. Many of us forget, or perhaps ignore, what this amazing power can do for us and for others. By training our minds on someone or something with a focused, unbiased attention, we can literally move mountains, tune into the vibrations of the universe, solve seemingly insurmountable problems, change our cellular composition, and heal ourselves and others. How does this work? Well, that remains a mystery.

The power of our consciousness, attuned, focused, funneled, and directed in open, accepting and unhindered attention, is the most powerful force we know of. Mystics throughout the ages, east and west, bear testimony to the universal power of mind. Through the directing of our attention, we can channel the universal mind, the pure mind, in a way that is less distorted and inhibited than through our usual brain transmitter transmission. Attention seems to clear the airwaves, provided of course it is directed to the right things. In mindfulness, the "right thing," in fact the only thing, is the present moment, as the present moment is all that truly exists.

We do not need to refer to the mystics to gain insight into the power of attention.

What will our children not do to get our attention? What animal, plant, or living thing will not respond to loving attention? Is there truly anything we cannot change if we give it loving attention?

Engaging with others requires our attention. Our undivided attention. This takes discipline, intention, and energy. The more we pay mindful attention, the clearer and more authentic our engagement will be. Our attention improves the quality of our experience and that of the other. Just think of the child who says: "Mommy, Mommy, watch… watch! You are not watching me!" The child knows when our attention strays or is distracted. He or she knows when we are not truly paying attention; when we are thinking of other things and are pretending. Imagine how much more we adults know and sense this.

Our attention, like a beam of energy, impacts the other and directly shapes both of our experiences. Half-hearted attention sets the unruly monkey-mind off on its mad pursuits to create disgruntled mischief. Half-hearted attention results in us misperceiving, misunderstanding, and disrespecting the other. Half-hearted attention redounds on our own experience of what is taking place in the present moment.

Disciplined attention is one of our greatest assets and our most powerful tools. Mindfulness, and especially meditation, helps us train and strengthen this tool and reminds us that it is there for a purpose, and that purpose is to improve our quality of engagement in everyday living. It truly is a gift not to be squandered.

Mindfulness is about giving the present moment loving attention. By loving we mean open-hearted, accepting, and inviting. When we pay attention in a mindfulness manner, all of us pays attention — our minds, our bodies, our souls. We give this minute everything we have got, all of it. From head to toe, from mind to body to soul. And we do this in this moment… and then the next… and then the next.

Attention is Limited

We also recognize that our attention is limited. Through practice and concentration exercises, meditation and mindfulness, we can develop our attention span, yet it is a limited resource. Our attention tires. It needs rest like that we get at that beach where we allow our minds to drift in the immersed, blended awareness of sheer sensation of all that is.

Even though we are focusing on our breath, meditation also gives our attention rest. Meditation is a gentle focus. It is a resting in the present moment as we breathe in and out. Nothing is required of us at that time other than to yield, let go, relax, be in the here and now. The neuroscientists tell us that meditation is one of the best ways to rest our brains, in some ways even better than sleep.

PRESENCE

Think of someone you know who has presence. What is it that is so arresting about this person? Is it not true that we are drawn to people with presence? We find something attractive about them that we desire for ourselves and that we would like to be associated with.

People with presence are typically at ease. They have poise, exude self-assurance, and have a dignified bearing. They seem internally and externally aligned. Body and mind work together synchronously. No disconnect is apparent. When they engage, they are present… they bring their presence to bear. They are all there!

Calm and alert attention is the foundation of presence. Open, non-judgmental, embodied attention is the hallmark of presence. When we are present we let things go and let the freshness of the new moment come into our experience. We see with fresh eyes, and hear with our hearts and our intuitions as much as our ears.

When we are present, we are engaged. We totally inhabit the present moment. We are living life as it unfolds. We are committed to treating each moment as a learning experience and each encounter as valuable and worthy. When we are present, we regulate our attention and our emotions, and we engage in each moment with equanimity.

Individuals—you and I—we need to commit ourselves to being present in all our actions in the world. CEOs and managers need to commit to role-modeling presence at work. The organizational culture should foster a spirit of presence thereby setting a foundation for a healthy, vibrant, and trusting culture of engagement.

WHAT MINDFULNESS TEACHES US

While our book has been focused largely on mindfulness at work, everything we have discussed is relevant to our entire lives. The person who goes to work, is also the person who comes home at night. When we leave in the morning, what mindfulness have we initiated? When we arrive home at night, what habitual, reactive, behaviors might we change?

As much as we kid ourselves that we are happier at the ball game than at the office, in life, there is no separation. Our mon-key-mind—full of drama—is always there, ball game or not, we are just not paying attention. Mindfulness helps us to calm this monkey-mind of ours wherever we are, giving us greater poise and dignity, both at the ball game and at work.

Mindfulness helps us to see that every moment is a defining moment, not just the dramatic ones. Every moment weaves the tapestry of our lives, and now we have a choice where we can take active part in that weaving. By being exquisitely attentive to each moment, we are fully alive to the present. We see, hear, and speak differently. We are attuned to what is going on at a core level, rather than leaving our half-attentive mind to make up some reality.

With mindfulness, we are present and attentive. We have an elegance. We are sensitive to timing. We are attuned to our own emotions and those of others. We communicate—which means we share—appropriately. That means in the right time, with the right people, about the right things, in the right way. We find we have more joy and more pleasure. We are more alert, alive and awake to the present. We are more helpful, more generous and more compassionate.

Mindfulness helps us to slow down, and choose our responses. We are less reactive and less mechanical. We are no longer programmed machines as we steadily dismantle our conditioned programming. We learn not to take everything personally; to non-identify and non-objectify. To simply let things be.

REMEMBERING MEDITATION

Meditation is foundational to mindfulness. As challenging as it might be for some of us, in the depths of our inner reflection is where we truly find the gold.

Besides the insights that meditation brings, which are significant, just ten minutes of meditation a day, changes one's physiology. It is the stress reliever par excellence, and it has an enormously positive impact on our brains. Meditation helps our breathing and our posture, both important contributors to our health.

So, whatever you do—try to find that ten minutes each day, day after day, to give to the inner you. Otherwise, as Viktor Frankl points out, if you do not go within, you will simply go without! And that would mean missing a great deal.

THE THREE QUESTIONS

There is only one time that is important: now
The most necessary person is the one with who you are: now
The most important affair is to do that person good: now
- Leo Tolstoy, The Three Questions

"It once occurred to a certain king that if he always knew the right time to begin everything, if he knew who were the right people to listen to, and whom to avoid, and, above all, if he always knew what was the most important thing to do, he would never fail in anything he might undertake.

The king proclaimed throughout his kingdom that he would give a great reward to anyone who would teach him the right time for every action, the most necessary people, and how he might know what was the most important thing to do.

Many learned men came to the king, but they all answered his questions differently. Still wishing to find the right answers to his questions, he decided to consult a hermit, widely renowned for his wisdom.

The hermit lived in a wood which he never quitted, and he received none but common folk. So, the king put on simple clothes and, before reaching the hermit's cell, dismounted from his horse. Leaving his bodyguard behind, he went on alone.

The king found the hermit digging and said to him: 'I have come to you, wise hermit, to ask you to answer three questions: How can I learn to do the right thing at the right time? Who are the people I most need, and to whom should I, therefore, pay more attention than to the rest? And, what affairs are the most important and need my first attention?'

The hermit listened to the king, but answered nothing. He just spat on his hand and recommenced digging. The king saw that the hermit was tired, and took over the digging.

Out of the blue, a person came running towards them. The man was injured and bleeding profusely. The king and the hermit tended to him and gave him water. Together they carried the wounded man into the hermit's hut and laid him on the bed. The king was so tired from his walk and from the work he had done, that he also fell asleep.

When he awoke in the morning, the strange bearded man lying on the bed was gazing intently at him. 'Forgive me!' said the bearded man in a weak voice, when he saw that the king was awake and was looking at him.

'You do not know me, but I know you. I am that enemy of yours who swore to revenge himself on you, because you executed my brother and seized his property. I knew you had gone alone to see the hermit, and I resolved to kill you on your way back. Your bodyguard, saw me in the woods, and they recognized me, and wounded me. I escaped from them and you have saved my life.'

The king was very glad to have made peace with his enemy so easily, and to have gained him for a friend, and he not only forgave him, but said he would send his servants and his own physician to attend him, and promised to restore his property.

The king then went out onto the porch and looked around for the hermit. Before going away, he wished once more to beg an answer to the questions he had put. The hermit was outside, sowing seeds in the beds that had been dug the day before.

The king approached him and said, 'For the last time, I pray you to answer my questions, wise man.'

'You have already been answered!' said the hermit, still crouching on his thin legs, and looking up at the king, who stood before him.

'How answered? What do you mean?' asked the king.

'Do you not see?' replied the hermit. 'If you had not pitied my weakness yesterday, and had not dug these beds for me, but had gone your way, that man would have attacked you, and you would have repented of not having stayed with me. So, the most important time was when you were digging the beds, and I was the most important man, and to do me good was your most important business.

Afterwards, when that man ran to us, the most important time was when you were attending to him, for if you had not bound up his wounds he would have died without having made peace with you. So, he was the most important man, and what you did for him was your most important business.

Remember then: there is only one time that is important — *now!* It is the most important time because it is the only time when we have any power. The most necessary person is the one with whom you are, for no man knows whether he will ever have dealings with anyone else, and the most important affair is to do that person good, because for that purpose alone was man sent into this life.'"

– Leo Tolstoy (1828-1910)

There is only one time that is important: now
The most necessary person is the one with whom you are: now
The most important affair is to do that person good: now

If we could practice a little more mindfulness each day, taking it moment by moment by moment, we would soon have a better me, a better you, a better world.

Appendix I

THE BODY SCAN

- Take an erect and relaxed posture in your seat with your feet flat on the floor
- Take a few slow deep breaths
- Feel a connection with your chair, and be aware of the room
- Allow yourself to take a moment to reflect and bring yourself present to yourself
- Your eyes are lowered, but slightly open to stave off drowsiness
- Begin by just feeling what you feel
- Allow yourself to feel everything you are feeling right now
- This is a way for you to come into direct contact with yourself
- It is a way to recognize that you do feel
- Mindfulness is the act of noticing
- Pay attention to the feeling of your breathing
- Feel its texture
- Feel the air on your body, the texture of your clothing, your aches and itches, the tensions and softness
- Take your awareness inside of your body, feel the fullness or emptiness of your belly, the beating of your heart and pulse, the tingles and buzz of aliveness happening every moment

- Take a few moments to do a scan of your body starting with the bottoms of your feet—being aware of sensations and noting what you notice
- Breathe into any tension you notice and let it soften
- Move attention to your legs... knees... thighs, again being aware of sensations and just noticing, then breathing into any tension or discomfort and allowing it to soften
- Then hips and pelvis... then up the spine slowly to the nape of the neck... aware of any sensations in the back
- Now attention to the front of the body... lower body through lower torso... chest to collar bone...sensations of muscles, skin, and organs inside
- Then neck and shoulders, allowing yourself to breathe and soften any tension
- Then jaw... face... being aware of any tension. Allow yourself to smile a little which helps relax the whole face
- Up the scalp to the crown of your head... notice sensations in your scalp and allow any tightness to soften
- With your body now relaxed and firm, the mind is a little quieter
- Allow your emotions to come to the surface and feel what you are feeling
- Feelings constantly pervade our life so we need to come in contact with them
- Whatever arises touch it lightly and let it go, just noticing
- Where do you feel your feelings? In your belly, in your shoulders? Behind your eyes? In your heart region? Pay attention to any sensations that accompany your emotions
- Feeling our feelings has an aspect of honesty and acceptance

- Feeling is the emotional connection that leads to the transformative aspect of mindfulness
- Feeling allows us to connect with the intuitive wisdom that resides in the messages our body is constantly sending us
- Now bring your attention gently back to feeling your body breathing
- Take a few slow deep breaths
- Feel yourself in your chair, feel the room around you
- Open your eyes fully and enjoy the enhanced integration of body and mind you have achieved

Appendix II

FURTHER READING

Leadership and Decision-Making

Beerel, Annabel. *Expert Systems in Business. Real World Applications*. Chichester, West Sussex, England: Ellis Horwood Limited, 1993.

Blake, Chris. *The Art of Decisions. How to Manage in an Uncertain World*. Upper Saddle River, New Jersey: Pearson Education, 2008.

Hammond, John S. et al. *Smart Choices. The Practical Guide to Making Better Life Decisions*. New York: Broadway Books, 1999.

Lehrer, Jonah. *How We Decide*. New York: Houghton Mifflin Harcourt, 2009.

March, James G. *A Primer on Decision Making*. New York: The Free Press, 1994.

Raffio, Thomas, with Barbara McLaughlin and Dave Cowens. *There are No Do-Overs: the Big Red Factors for Sustaining a Business Long Term*. Raleigh, NC: Curran Pendleton Press, 2013.

Ruggiero, Vincent Ryan. *The Art of Thinking*. New York: Pearson-Longman, 2006.

Russo, J. Edward & Paul J.H. Schoemaker. *Winning Decisions. Getting it Right the First Time*. New York: Currency Doubleday, 2002.

Meditation

Chaudhuri, Haridas. *The Philosophy of Meditation*. New York: Philosophical Library, 1965.

Chodron, Pema. *How to Meditate*. Boulder, Colorado: Sounds True, 2013.

Goleman, Daniel. *The Meditative Mind*. New York: Jeremy Tarcher/Putnam Book, 1977.

Hagen, Steve. *Meditation. Now or Never*. New York; HarperCollins, 2007.

Humphreys, Christmas. *Concentration and Meditation*. Rockport, MA: Element, 1998.

Kempton, Sally. *Meditation for the Love of It*. Boulder, Colorado: Sounds True, 2011.

Kornfield, Jack. *Meditation for Beginners*. Boulder, Colorado: Sounds True, Inc., 2008.

Main, John. *The Way of Unknowing*. London, U.K.: Darton, Longman, and Todd, 1990.

Nairn, Rob. *What is Meditation? Buddhism for Everyone*. Boston, MA: Shambhala, 1999.

Rosenberg, Larry with David Guy. *Breath by Breath. The Liberating Practice of Insight Meditation*. Boston, MA: Shambhala, 2004.

Salzberg, Sharon. *Real Happiness. The Power of Meditation*. New York: Workman Publishing Company, Inc., 2011.

Smith, Jean, editor. *Breath Sweeps Mind. A First Guide to Meditation Practice*. New York: Riverhead Books, 1998.

Mind and Brain

Falk, Dean. *Braindance. New Discoveries about Human Origins and Brain Evolution.* New York: Henry Holt and Company, Inc., 1992.

Hanson, Rick, PhD., with Richard Mendius, MD. *Buddha's Brain. The Practical Neuroscience of Happiness, Love, & Wisdom.* Oakland, CA: New Harbinger Publications, Inc., 2009.

Newberg, Andrew, MD., and Mark Robert Waldman. *How Enlightenment Changes Your Brain.* New York: Penguin Random House, 2016.

Rock, David. *Your Brain at Work.* New York: Harper Business, 2009.

Siegel, Daniel J. *The Mindful Brain.* New York: W.W. Norton & Company, 2007.

Siegel, Daniel J. *Mindsight. The New Science of Personal Transformation.* New York: Bantam Books, 2011.

Mindfulness

Boorstein, Sylvia, Ph.D., *Happiness is an Inside Job.* New York; Ballantine Books, 2008.

Chodron, Pema. *Start Where You Are. A Guide to Compassionate Living.* Boston, MA: Shambhala, 1994.

Gunaratana, Bhante Henepola. *Mindfulness in Plain English.* Boston, MA: Wisdom Publications, 2002.

Hahn, Thich Nhat. *The Miracle of Mindfulness.* Boston, MA: Beacon Press, 1987.

Hougaard, Rasmus with J. Carter and Gillian Coutts. *One Second Ahead.* New York: Palgrave Macmillan, 2016.

Kabat-Zinn, Jon. *Full Catastrophe Living.* New York: Bantam Books, 2013.

Langer, Ellen. *Mindfulness.* Reading, MA: Perseus Books, 1989.

Index